lazy days
and beach blankets

lazy days
and beach blankets

Simple alfresco dining with family and friends

RYLAND
PETERS
& SMALL

LONDON NEW YORK

First published in the UK in 2009
by Ryland Peters & Small
20–21 Jockey's Fields
London WC1R 4BW
www.rylandpeters.com

10 9 8 7 6 5 4 3 2 1

Text © Ghillie Basan, Fiona Beckett, Susannah
Blake, Maxine Clark, Ross Dobson, Clare Ferguson,
Liz Franklin, Tonia George, Brian Glover, Jane
Noraika, Louise Pickford, Ben Reed, Fiona Smith,
Sunil Vijayakar, Fran Warde, Lindy Wildsmith and
Ryland Peters & Small 2009

Design and photographs
© Ryland Peters & Small 2009

ISBN: 978 1 84597 844 0

A catalogue record for this book is available from
the British Library.

Printed and bound in China.

Notes

• All spoon measurements are level, unless
otherwise stated.

• Eggs are medium unless otherwise specified.
Uncooked or partially cooked eggs should not
be served to the very old, frail, young children,
pregnant women or those with compromised
immune systems.

• To sterilize preserving jars, wash them in hot,
soapy water and rinse in boiling water. Place in
a large pan and cover with hot water. With the
lid on, bring the water to the boil and boil for
15 minutes. Turn off the heat and leave the jars
in the hot water until just before they are to be
filled. Invert the jars onto kitchen paper to dry.
Sterilize the lids for 5 minutes, by boiling, or
follow the manufacturer's instructions. Jars
should be filled and sealed while still hot.

Design Toni Kay and Paul Tilby
Editor Helen Ridge
Picture Research Emily Westlake
Production Toby Marshall
Art Director Leslie Harrington
Publishing Director Alison Starling

Indexer Hilary Bird

contents

Parasols and picnic rugs

Lazy days outside are meant to be hassle-free and all about enjoying good company, simple food and thirst-quenching drinks. This book is designed to give you plenty of inspiration for meals, snacks, cocktails and summery settings to help you make the most of glorious sun-filled afternoons and long, balmy evenings. Here are a few helpful tips if you are planning to eat alfresco with family and friends:

• Depending on the number of guests you are expecting, you will need extra chairs and a large table, plus plates, cutlery and glasses. All these things can be hired if you need to.

• Choosing what to cook is the fun part – try to offer a balance of meat, poultry, fish and seafood, vegetables and vegetarian alternatives.

• Plan well ahead so you can order ingredients in advance. Shop for the non-perishables a week ahead and then many of the raw ingredients can be bought the day before and others picked up early on the day of the party.

• If you are having a barbecue, always check that you have plenty of fuel (unless you have a mains gas or electric grill). Keep a spare full gas bottle or buy double the amount of charcoal you need—you can always use it next time.

• Order drinks in advance and don't forget to ask for 'sale or return' – over-order rather than under-order. The same supplier may be used to hire glasses. Order lots of non-alcoholic drinks as well, for non-drinkers and children.

• Food and drink must be kept cold, so make as much room in the refrigerator as you can for the food – line up the cool boxes for salads, and hire dustbins or plastic tubs for drinks and fill them up with ice. Have the drinks delivered cold, and pack them in ice as soon as they arrive.

• Evening parties need plenty of night lights, storm lanterns and large candles to add a lovely ambience to the evening.

• Burning citronella candles and mosquito coils will help to keep the bugs at bay.

• If you are barbecuing, find a sheltered spot with little or no wind to blow smoke and sparks, but close enough to the kitchen for convenience. Choose a flat non-flammable surface, such as a terrace or flat grassy area. Avoid a wooden deck as sparks or embers may drop through.

• To ensure that what we eat is safe for us we must take the steps necessary to avoid food poisoning which, although rarely life-threatening, can be extremely unpleasant. Young children, the elderly, and pregnant women are particularly vulnerable to illness caused by unsafe foods, and the main way that food becomes contaminated is by poor storage or dirty utensils.

• Keep foods covered with clingfilm while they are waiting to be cooked to keep the bugs away.

• All cooked foods are safest eaten soon after cooking and most barbecued foods are best eaten hot from the fire. If you are barbecuing vegetables to eat later, then cool them as quickly as possible and chill in the refrigerator until required.

• Remember health issues when cooking pork and poultry, always make sure the meat is totally cooked through before eating. This can be done either by using an instant-read thermometer or by inserting a skewer into the thickest part of the meat. If the juices run clear, the meat is cooked. If they are bloody, return to the hob or barbecue and continue cooking.

snacks & sides

This is a fun version of garlic bread, and the slightly smoky flavour from the coals is delicious. You can also add cubes of cheese such as mozzarella or fontina to the skewers.

garlic bread skewers

1 baguette

150 ml extra virgin olive oil

2 garlic cloves, crushed

2 tablespoons chopped fresh parsley

sea salt and freshly ground black pepper

6–8 wooden skewers, soaked in water for 30 minutes

Serves 6–8

Preheat the barbecue.

Cut the bread into 2 cm thick slices, then cut the slices crossways to make half moons.

Put the olive oil, garlic, parsley, salt and pepper into a large bowl, add the bread and toss until well coated with the parsley and oil.

Thread the garlic bread onto skewers and cook over medium-hot coals for 2–3 minutes on each side until toasted.

Variation Cut 250 g mozzarella cheese into about 24 small pieces. Thread a piece of bread onto the skewer and continue to alternate the cheese and bread. Cook as in the main recipe.

dried tomato purée

Made from sun-dried and kiln-dried tomatoes, this paste has an intense, sweet-sharp taste, enlivening soups and sauces, as well as adding new interest to the appetizer tray.

100 g sun-dried or kiln-dried tomatoes

2 tablespoons extra virgin olive oil

4 garlic cloves, peeled

1 teaspoon coarse sea salt

1/2 teaspoon dried oregano or rosemary, crumbled

1 teaspoon fennel or anise seeds

90 ml boiling water or vegetable stock

4 tablespoons dry white wine

crudités, young salad leaves, toasts or hard-boiled egg halves, to serve

Serves 4

Scissor-snip the tomatoes into small pieces. Heat the olive oil in a frying pan and add the tomatoes.

Pound together the garlic, salt, oregano and fennel seeds using a pestle and mortar. Add to the tomatoes and stir over high heat until aromatic. Pour in the boiling liquid and cook over medium heat, stirring, for a further minute, until most of the liquid has evaporated. Turn off the heat. Add the wine, then cover and leave for 5 minutes.

Tip the pan contents into a food processor and whizz until the mixture becomes a rough paste, about 15–20 seconds. Leave to cool.

Spoon the paste into one or more serving dishes. Smooth the surface and chill.

Serve with crudités, young salad leaves, toasts or hard-boiled egg halves.

green olive and basil paste

This unusual Provençal-style paste is delicious, especially when spread on crisp biscuits and served with a glass of something chilled. It's also very easy to make.

250 g green olives stuffed with anchovies in brine or 250 g stoned green olives in brine and 4 tinned anchovy fillets

2 garlic cloves, chopped

half a handful of fresh basil leaves, torn into pieces

25 g stale bread, wetted and squeezed dry

60 ml extra virgin olive oil

1–2 teaspoons white wine vinegar (optional)

salted crackers, tiny oven-dried ficelle toasts, small crispbreads or baby cos lettuce leaves, to serve

Serves 4–6

Put all the ingredients except the oil and vinegar into a food processor. Whizz for 30 seconds.

With the machine running, drizzle in enough olive oil to create a pleasant texture.

Taste, add vinegar to season, if liked, then do a final burst of processing to combine.

Serve with salted crackers, tiny oven-dried ficelle toasts or small crispbreads. Baby cos lettuce leaves are another option.

Variation Substitute the chopped leaves from 8 stems of fresh French tarragon for the basil.

Black, glossy tapenade gets its name from *tapeña*, the Provençal word for 'caper'. This essential ingredient, along with salted anchovies, tinned tuna (optional), garlic, herbs, olive oil, *marc* (*eau de vie*) or lemon juice or both, creates a heady mix. Use tapenade on toast, and eat with hard-boiled egg halves and raw carrot, celery, fennel, cucumber and tomato. It also makes a good sauce for poached fish or steaks. These days, green olives, sweet peppers and sun-dried tomatoes often go into so-called tapenades, but black olives create the true classic.

tapenade

350 g dry-cured, soft black olives (to yield 250 g stoned olives)

100 g salted capers, rinsed

6 fresh salted anchovies, boned, rinsed and chopped, or 12 tinned anchovy fillets, chopped

50 g tinned tuna in brine, drained and flaked

2–4 garlic cloves, crushed

1 teaspoon mixed dried herbs, including thyme, oregano, lavender and savory

1/2 teaspoon coarse sea salt

freshly ground black pepper

60–90 ml extra virgin olive oil

1 tablespoon marc de Provence (eau de vie)

freshly squeezed juice of 1/4 lemon (optional)

garlicky toasts and rocket leaves, to serve

Serves 4–6

Stone the olives and put in a food processor with the capers, anchovies and tuna. Process, in bursts, to a pulp.

Put the garlic, herbs, salt and pepper into a large mortar, and pound with a pestle to create a pungent paste. Gradually work in the olive pulp, then process in bursts, with the oil, until creamy.

Taste and add the marc and the lemon juice, if liked, for balance.

Drizzle the mixture over garlicky toasts and top with rocket leaves. Alternatively, serve with grilled fish or roast lamb, or mixed into butter for grilled steaks.

Aubergines of all sizes, colours and shapes are the glory of market stalls throughout Provence; every cook can afford this ingredient. The joky title of this recipe implies (justifiably) that aubergines are precious in their own right. Local cooks roast them in the oven or over charcoal but they can also be grilled directly over gas flames, spiked between two forks.

beggar's caviar

2 medium aubergines (about 500 g in total)

2 garlic cloves, crushed

3 tinned salted anchovy fillets

60 ml extra virgin olive oil

sea salt and freshly ground black pepper

torn fresh basil or scissor-snipped lovage or flat leaf parsley (optional), to garnish

crusty bread or small toasts, to serve

Serves 4–6

Preheat the grill and position an oven rack about 7.5 cm below the heat source.

Pierce each aubergine six times or so with a fork, then place on the rack. Cook for 10 minutes. Turn over and cook for a further 10 minutes. Alternatively, push kitchen forks into both ends of each aubergine, turn the gas hob to its highest and flame-grill each aubergine, turning at intervals so that they are evenly charred, hot and cooked through, about 6 minutes each. Leave to cool.

Peel off most of the aubergine skin and discard the leafy stem ends. Drain off any juice.

Put the garlic, anchovies, salt and pepper in a mortar and pound together with a pestle. Add about a quarter of an aubergine and continue to pound.

Transfer the mixture and all the remaining aubergine flesh to a food processor. Pulse briefly in half-a-dozen 5-second bursts, drizzling in the olive oil at intervals. This will create an earthy-textured paste.

Taste and season again. Spoon into a serving dish, sprinkle with your preferred fresh herb, then serve warm or cool, with crusty bread or small toasts.

Hot from the barbecue, this aromatic herb bread is delicious eaten on its own with olive oil for dipping.

barbecued rosemary flatbread

250 g strong white flour, plus extra for dusting

1½ teaspoons easy-blend dried yeast

1 teaspoon salt

1 tablespoon chopped fresh rosemary

120 ml hot water

2 tablespoons extra virgin olive oil, plus extra for brushing

Serves 4

Preheat the barbecue to low.

Sift the flour into the bowl of an electric mixer and stir in the yeast, salt and rosemary. Add the hot water and olive oil and knead with the dough hook at high speed for about 8 minutes or until the dough is smooth and elastic. Alternatively, sift the flour into a large bowl and stir in the yeast, salt and rosemary. Make a well in the centre, then add the hot water and olive oil and mix to form a soft dough. Turn out onto a lightly floured work surface and knead until the dough is smooth and elastic.

Shape the dough into a ball, then put into an oiled bowl, cover with a tea towel and leave to rise in a warm place for 45–60 minutes or until doubled in size.

Punch down the dough and divide into 4. Roll each piece out on a lightly floured work surface to make a 15 cm long oval.

Brush the bread with a little olive oil and barbecue for 5 minutes, then brush the top with the remaining olive oil, flip and barbecue for a further 4–5 minutes until the bread is cooked through.

Serve hot with olive oil for dipping.

sun-dried tomato, olive and basil bread

175 g plain flour

1 tablespoon baking powder

3 large eggs

100 ml milk

100 ml olive oil

100 g mature Gruyère cheese, grated

100 g sun-dried tomatoes in oil, drained and roughly chopped

60 g stoned black olives marinated with herbs, roughly chopped

a small handful of basil leaves, roughly sliced

sea salt and freshly ground black pepper

a 21 x 11-cm non-stick loaf tin, lightly greased and floured

Serves 6

These easy breads are very popular in France where they are somewhat confusingly called 'cake'. They're like a cross between a savoury bread and a quiche, and delicious to nibble with drinks.

Preheat the oven to 180°C (350°F) Gas 4.

Sift the flour with the baking powder and season well with salt and black pepper. Whisk the eggs and whisk in the milk and oil. Tip two-thirds of the liquid into the flour, beat well, then add the remaining liquid. Mix in the Gruyère, tomatoes, olives and basil, then tip into the prepared loaf tin. Bake in the preheated oven for 50 minutes or until a skewer comes out clean. Leave to cool, then remove from the tin. Wrap in aluminium foil and keep in the fridge.

Serve at room temperature, sliced and cut into halves or squares. You could also serve a plate of some chunky handcut, slices of salami that can be eaten with your fingers.

toasted ciabatta pizzas

Other breads can be used in these fantastic, fresh-tasting pizzas, so don't go shopping specially for ciabatta. You can also use Cheddar or blue cheese instead of mozzarella.

1 loaf ciabatta, split lengthways or sliced

1 garlic clove, peeled

about 4 tablespoons olive oil

4 ripe tomatoes, skinned and sliced

a handful of stoned olives

a bunch of marjoram

2 balls mozzarella cheese

a bunch of basil

sea salt and freshly ground black pepper

Serves 4

Preheat the oven to 180°C (350°F) Gas 4.

Grill the ciabatta under a hot grill until lightly toasted, then rub with the garlic, using it like a grater. Put the garlic ciabatta on a baking tray and drizzle with a little of the olive oil.

Arrange the sliced tomatoes on the bread, then add the olives, marjoram, mozzarella, basil, salt and pepper. Drizzle more oil over the top.

Cook in the preheated oven for 15–20 minutes until the tomatoes are softened and crisp round the edges and the mozzarella has melted.

three salsas

Salsas give an extra dimension to chicken, meat and fish and are incredibly versatile. The hot pineapple and papaya salsa is good with prawns or pork, the creamy corn salsa marries well with chicken, while the tomato and ginger salsa is very good with white fish or tortilla chips.

creamy corn salsa

1 corn-on-the-cob, husk removed

2 red chillies

1 tomato, diced

1 garlic clove, crushed

freshly squeezed juice of 1/2 lime

1 tablespoon maple syrup

2 tablespoons soured cream

sea salt and freshly ground black pepper

Serves 6

Preheat a barbecue until hot.

Add the corn and cook for about 15 minutes, turning frequently, until charred on all sides. Leave to cool.

Add the chillies and grill until the skins are charred all over. Transfer to a bowl and cover with a clean cloth until cool.

Using a sharp knife, cut down all sides of the corn cob to remove the kernels. Put them into a bowl. Peel and deseed the chillies, chop the flesh and add it to the corn.

Stir in all the remaining ingredients, season to taste, then serve.

hot pineapple and papaya salsa

1/2 ripe pineapple

1/2 large papaya

freshly squeezed juice of 1 lime

1–2 green chillies, deseeded and finely chopped

2 spring onions, finely chopped

1 tablespoon chopped fresh mint

1 tablespoon Thai fish sauce

Serves 6

Peel the pineapple, remove and discard the core, then dice the flesh and put into a serving bowl, together with any juice.

Peel the papaya, scoop out the seeds and dice the flesh. Add to the pineapple.

Stir in the spring onions, mint and fish sauce, set aside to infuse for about 30 minutes, then serve.

tomato, sesame and ginger salsa

2 ripe tomatoes, peeled, deseeded and diced

1/2 red onion, finely chopped

5 cm fresh ginger, peeled and grated

1 garlic clove, chopped

1 tablespoon chopped fresh coriander

2 tablespoons peanut oil

1 tablespoon soy sauce

1 teaspoon sesame oil

Serves 6

Put all the ingredients into a bowl, set aside to infuse for about 30 minutes, then serve.

400 g dried skinned broad beans

1 fresh bouquet garni of parsley, celery, bay leaf and thyme

1 large onion, coarsely chopped

1 potato, unpeeled

4 garlic cloves, chopped

60 ml extra virgin olive oil, plus extra to serve (optional)

freshly squeezed juice of 1 lemon

6 sprigs of fresh oregano, chopped

sea salt and freshly ground black pepper

your choice of baby leafy vegetables, radishes, crusty bread, cucumber, to serve

Serves 4

All round the Mediterranean, fresh and dried peas, beans and lentils are used in dips and spreads, as sauces with pasta and in soups. Depending on the region and local herbs, different flavours and ingredients are used. Near Nice, Swiss chard stems and parsley may be added; in Italy, rosemary is used rather than oregano; and in North African immigrant communities, mint may be an option. The constant is dried broad beans. The best are the skinless type: they cook quickly, taste better and have a more delicate texture. Soak them for 4 hours or overnight in cold water, or cheat by putting them in a saucepan, covering them with boiling water, bringing them to the boil and soaking for 2 hours with the heat turned off. Drain, cover with cold water, bring to the boil and simmer until tender. Drain again, season and use as a dip or spread (or dilute as a sauce or soup).

italian bean dip

Soak and drain the beans as described above, then put them in a large saucepan with the bunch of herbs, onion and potato and add 2 litres boiling water. Bring to the boil, boil hard for 10 minutes, reduce the heat and cook, part-covered for 1½–2 hours or until you can crush the beans easily with your thumbnail.

Drain the vegetables and discard the herbs. Working in batches if necessary, put the beans, potato, onion and garlic in a food processor, with the olive oil, lemon juice, oregano, salt and pepper. Blend in short bursts to a grainy but creamy purée.

Serve hot (as a side dish), warm or cool, sprinkled with extra olive oil. Serve as a dip or spread with baby leafy vegetables, radishes and cucumber or with bread chunks, or a combination.

200 g for each serving of fresh, young, summer vegetables, washed and trimmed, such as baby carrots, baby fennel bulbs, radishes, cherry tomatoes, baby courgettes

Bagna cauda

50 g unsalted butter

3–4 large garlic cloves, crushed

50 g anchovies in oil, drained and chopped

200 ml extra virgin olive oil

Serves 4–6

summer vegetables
with bagna cauda

Put the bagna cauda – the 'hot bath' – of warm anchovy butter in the centre of the table with a basket of fresh summer vegetables, so everyone can just help themselves.

Arrange the trimmed vegetables in a basket or on a large platter.

To make the bagna cauda, put the butter and garlic into a small saucepan and heat gently. Simmer very slowly for 4–5 minutes until the garlic has softened, but not browned. Add the anchovies, stir well, then pour in the oil. Cook gently for a further 10 minutes, stirring occasionally, until the sauce is soft and almost creamy.

Transfer the sauce to a dish and serve at once with the selection of trimmed vegetables.

18 small artichokes

1 lemon, halved

2 tablespoons extra virgin olive oil

sea salt and freshly ground black pepper

lime wedges, to serve

Chilli lime mayonnaise

1 dried chipotle chilli

2 egg yolks

300 ml olive oil

freshly squeezed juice of 1 lime

sea salt

Serves 6

Small or baby artichokes are best for this dish because they can be barbecued without any blanching first.

barbecued artichokes
with chilli lime mayonnaise

To make the mayonnaise, cover the dried chilli with boiling water and leave to soak for 30 minutes. Drain and pat dry, then cut in half and scrape out the seeds. Finely chop the flesh and put into a food processor. Add the egg yolks and a little salt and blend briefly until frothy. With the blade running, drizzle the oil through the funnel until the sauce is thick and glossy. Add the lime juice and, if the mayonnaise is too thick, a tablespoon of warm water. Taste and adjust the seasoning, then cover and set aside.

Preheat the barbecue.

Trim the stalks from the artichokes and cut off the top 2 cm of the globes. Slice the globes in half lengthways, cutting out the central 'choke', if necessary. Rub the cut surfaces all over with lemon juice to stop them discolouring.

Toss the artichokes with the oil and a little salt and pepper. Barbecue over medium-hot coals for 15–20 minutes, depending on size, until charred and tender, turning halfway through the cooking time. Serve with the mayonnaise and wedges of lime.

Gooey, caramelized garlic spread over lightly chargrilled toast is the perfect outdoor starter for keeping your guests happy while you're finalizing the lunch preparations.

bruschetta
with caramelized garlic

1 whole head of garlic

a sprig of fresh thyme

1 tablespoon extra virgin olive oil, plus extra to sprinkle

4 slices sourdough or ciabatta bread

sea salt and freshly ground black pepper

Serves 4

Preheat the barbecue.

Cut the top off the garlic head to reveal the cloves. Put the head onto a piece of foil, add the thyme sprig and season with salt and pepper. Sprinkle with the olive oil, then fold over the foil, sealing the edges to form a parcel. Cook over hot coals for about 20 minutes or until the garlic is softened.

Put the bread slices on a barbecue rack and toast for a few minutes on each side. Squeeze the cooked garlic out of the cloves and spread onto the toasted bread. Sprinkle with a little more olive oil, season with salt and pepper and serve while still warm.

Variation Try topping the garlic with slices of Camembert cheese and sprinkle with extra virgin olive oil.

coriander flatbreads
with spiced aubergines and split pea dip

Give yourself plenty of time to make the bread, and try to time the last batch of baking so that the aromas leave your guests in no doubt that the bread is homemade. Serve with a salad of tomato, red onion and herbs.

Preheat the oven to 200°C (400°F) Gas 6.

To make the flatbreads, put the flour in a large bowl, then stir in the yeast, salt, cumin seeds, coriander and chilli. Make a well in the centre and add the water. Mix with your hands to form a dough. Either transfer to an electric mixer fitted with a dough hook or continue kneading by hand for about 10 minutes or until the dough is smooth and springy to the touch. Return to the bowl, lightly brush the top with oil, then cover with clingfilm. Leave to rise in a warm place for 30–40 minutes.

To make the spiced aubergines, put the lemon juice, chilli, mint, olive oil, salt and pepper in a blender and process until smooth. Put the aubergines and red onions on the baking tray. Pour the olive oil mixture over the vegetables and massage in well with your hands. Bake in the preheated oven for 30 minutes, then transfer to a serving bowl and top with the parsley. Turn up the oven temperature to 230°C (450°F) Gas 8.

To make the dip, put the yellow split peas in a medium saucepan, then cover with cold water and add the salt. Bring to the boil and cook for 30–40 minutes until soft. Drain, then transfer to a food processor. Add the cumin, lemon juice, garlic and olive oil and blend to a smooth purée. Add salt and pepper to taste, then transfer to a bowl and sprinkle with extra olive oil and some dill.

Meanwhile, to cook the flatbreads, transfer the dough to a lightly floured work surface and knead for a few minutes. Divide into 20–25 balls. Using a rolling pin, roll the dough balls into thin, flat ovals. Put on a lightly greased baking tray and cook in batches in the preheated oven for 15–20 minutes until golden and puffy. Serve with the aubergines and split pea dip and a salad of tomato, red onion and herbs.

Coriander flatbreads

750 g strong white bread flour, plus extra for dusting

7 g sachet easy-blend dried yeast

2 teaspoons sea salt

1 tablespoon cumin seeds, lightly toasted in a dry frying pan

a large handful of fresh coriander, chopped

1 red chilli, deseeded and finely chopped

about 1 litre tepid water

olive oil, for brushing

Spiced aubergines

freshly squeezed juice of 1 lemon

1 red chilli, deseeded and chopped

a large handful of fresh mint leaves, finely chopped

100 ml olive oil

3 aubergines, cut into chunks

1 red onion, cut into wedges

fresh flat leaf parsley, chopped, to serve

sea salt and freshly ground black pepper

Split pea dip

300 g yellow split peas

1 teaspoon sea salt

1 teaspoon cumin seeds, lightly toasted in a dry frying pan, then ground in a coffee grinder

freshly squeezed juice of 1 lemon

2 garlic cloves, crushed

4 tablespoons olive oil, plus extra to serve

fresh dill, coarsely chopped, to serve

sea salt and freshly ground black pepper

1–2 large baking trays, lightly greased

Serves 4

Topping

2 tablespoons olive oil

2 large sweet onions (about 500 g in total), thinly sliced

1 garlic clove, finely chopped

1 teaspoon finely chopped thyme or
1/2 teaspoon dried thyme

150 g small stoned marinated black olives

sea salt and freshly ground black pepper

a few small basil leaves, to garnish

Pastry

100 g Quark or curd cheese

100 g unsalted butter, cut into cubes, at room temperature

125 g plain flour

1 teaspoon baking powder

a good pinch of salt

an 8-cm pastry cutter

2 x 12-hole shallow tartlet tins

Makes about 12–14

mini pissaladières

These tartlets make a sophisticated and popular addition to any picnic. They can also be made in advance, frozen and then reheated from frozen in a moderate oven, which all helps to take the pressure off you on the day.

Heat the oil in a large flameproof casserole or saucepan. Tip in the onions, then cook over medium heat until they have begun to collapse (about 10 minutes). Stir in the garlic and thyme, turn the heat down a little and continue to cook for another 30–40 minutes until the onions are soft and golden and any liquid has evaporated, taking care that they don't catch and burn. Season with salt and pepper and set aside to cool.

While the onions are cooking, make the pastry. Tip the Quark into a food processor with the softened butter and process until smooth. Sift the flour with the baking powder and salt and add to the creamed cheese and butter in 2 batches, using the pulse to incorporate it. Once the mixture starts to form a ball, turn it out of the processor onto a floured board and form it into a flat disc. Put it in a plastic bag and chill for an hour in the fridge.

When ready to make the tartlets, preheat the oven to 220°C (425°F) Gas 7. Roll out the pastry quite thinly. Stamp rounds out of the pastry, re-rolling the offcuts as necessary, and lay them in the hollows of the tartlet tins. Spoon in teaspoonfuls of the cooled onion mixture and top with an olive. Bake for 15–20 minutes until the pastry is puffed up and golden.

Cool for 10 minutes, then remove the tarts carefully from the tin and arrange on a plate. Scatter with a few small basil leaves and serve.

turkish toasted bread

Asian food shops usually stock a wide variety of unusual and delicious items, including a range of different breads that can be used for this recipe.

Preheat the oven to 170°C (325°F) Gas 3.

Put the harissa, coriander, olive oil, olives and chillies in a small bowl and mix well. Divide the mixture between the pieces of bread, then sandwich the halves back together.

Put on a baking tray and cook in the preheated oven for 10 minutes. Remove and serve hot.

* Harissa paste is a hot blend of chillies and spices available from Middle Eastern stores, delicatessens and some supermarkets. It's great to have on hand for firing up all sorts of dishes. Stir it into couscous or mix with yoghurt and serve as a dip for crudités.

1 teaspoon harissa paste*

a bunch of fresh coriander, chopped

2 tablespoons olive oil

50 g stoned olives, chopped

2 red chillies, deseeded and chopped

4 slices small Turkish flatbread, pita bread or small flour tortillas, separated into discs

a baking tray

Serves 4

stuffed focaccia bread

This superb focaccia really does not take too long to prepare, and the aroma is totally beguiling.

500 g strong white bread flour

7 g sachet easy-blend dried yeast

1 tablespoon olive oil, plus extra to brush

sea salt

small sprigs of fresh rosemary

Filling

1/2 red pepper, halved, deseeded and sliced

1/2 orange pepper, halved, deseeded and sliced

1 red onion, sliced

olive oil, for roasting

200 g mozzarella cheese, cut into cubes

a large handful of fresh basil, chopped

8 sun-dried tomatoes in oil, sliced, plus 1 tablespoon of the oil

a handful of stoned black olives

sea salt and freshly ground black pepper

a baking tray, lightly greased and floured

Serves 6–8

Preheat the oven to 180°C (350°F) Gas 4.

To make the dough, put the flour, 1 teaspoon salt and the yeast in a large bowl. Stir in the olive oil and 350 ml water, then bring the dough together with your hands. Knead the dough by hand until it has a smooth, springy consistency (this should take about 10 minutes) or transfer to a machine with a dough hook attachment. Return to the bowl and lightly oil the top to prevent it from drying out. Cover with clingfilm or a damp tea towel and leave to rise in a warm place for 30 minutes until doubled in size.

Meanwhile, to prepare the filling, put the peppers and onion in a roasting tin, sprinkle with olive oil and salt and roast in the preheated oven for 15 minutes. Remove from the oven and leave to cool. Transfer to a bowl, add the mozzarella, basil, tomatoes, oil, olives, salt and pepper and mix well.

When the dough has risen to double its original size, transfer to a lightly floured surface and cut in half. Roll out the first half to the size of the baking tray and use to line the tray. Spread the filling over the top, leaving a 2.5 cm border around the edge. Roll out the remaining dough and put on top of the filling. Press the edges of the dough together to seal.

Brush with the 2 teaspoons olive oil, sprinkle with sea salt and dot with sprigs of rosemary, then leave to rise for a further 30 minutes. Just before cooking, use your thumb to make lots of indentations in the dough – this looks very attractive when cooked. Bake in the preheated oven for 40 minutes until lightly golden.

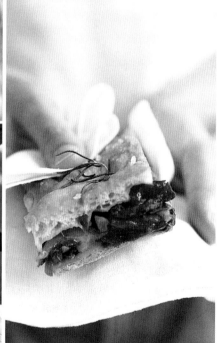

Chicken Caesar salad has travelled all over the world and many additions to the basic lettuce and croutons with cheese and anchovy dressing can be found. This variation, wrapped in a tortilla, is a great idea for a picnic dish.

chicken caesar wrap

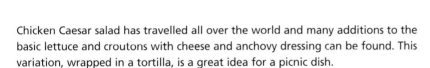

Grill or fry the bacon for 2–3 minutes until crisp. Cool, then cut into thin strips. Roughly shred the chicken into large strips.

To make the dressing, put the egg yolk into a small bowl, add the lemon juice, Worcestershire sauce and a little salt and pepper and whisk until frothy. Gradually whisk in the oil, a little at a time, until thickened and glossy. Add 2 tablespoons water to thin the sauce, then stir in the cheese.

Lay the tortilla flat on a work surface and arrange a little lettuce down the middle of each one. Top with chicken, bacon, anchovies, a spoonful of the dressing and, finally, more lettuce. Wrap the tortilla into a roll, then wrap the roll in a napkin. Repeat to make 6 wraps. Serve immediately or chill to serve later.

3 large slices of smoked bacon

250 g cooked chicken breast

6 small flour tortillas

300 g cos lettuce, shredded (inner leaves only)

12 anchovy fillets in oil, drained and chopped

Caesar dressing

1 egg yolk

1 tablespoon freshly squeezed lemon juice

1 teaspoon Worcestershire sauce

150 ml olive oil

25 g freshly grated Parmesan cheese

sea salt and freshly ground black pepper

Serves 6

2 red peppers, left whole

4 small focaccia or Turkish rolls, halved

2 large, cooked chicken breasts, shredded

a small handful of baby spinach

Rocket aïoli

1 egg yolk

1 teaspoon white wine vinegar

a bunch of rocket, about 50 g, coarsely chopped

1 garlic clove, crushed

150 ml olive oil

sea salt and freshly ground black pepper

Serves 4

Panini, which is Italian for toasted sandwiches, can be prepared ahead of time, then cooked just before you want to serve them. The combination of chargrilled peppers, tender chicken and a delicious rocket aïoli is definitely hard to beat.

chicken panini
with roasted pepper and rocket aïoli

Preheat the barbecue, then cook the peppers over hot coals or grill for about 20 minutes until charred all over. Put into a plastic bag and leave to cool. Peel off the skin and discard the seeds, then cut the flesh into strips.

To make the aïoli, put the egg yolk, vinegar and a little salt and pepper into a food processor and blend briefly until frothy. Add the rocket and garlic and pulse for 30 seconds. With the machine still running, gradually pour in the olive oil until the sauce is thickened and speckled with vivid green. Taste and adjust the seasoning.

Spread a little of the rocket aïoli onto the cut sides of each roll and fill the rolls with the chicken, pepper strips and spinach leaves. Press the halves together.

Preheat the flat plate on the barbecue and cook the panini over low heat for 4–5 minutes, then, using tongs, flip over and cook the other side for a further 5 minutes until toasted. If you don't have a flat plate, cook in a ridged stove-top grill pan, either on the barbecue, or on the stove. Serve hot.

In Sicily, this is known as *cabbucio*, meaning hood or cowl, and refers to a kind of bruschetta with a lid. Authentic Italian bread is still additive-free, which means it goes stale quickly, but put yesterday's uncut loaf in a hot oven for a few minutes and it will come out like new. Cut it open while hot and anoint it with extra virgin oil and your chosen filling and you have a delicious snack. Alternatively, you can use fresh bread.

hot crusty loaf filled with mozzarella, salami and tomato

500 g bloomer or fresh 'flat' crusty Italian loaf

5 large tomatoes, thinly sliced

200 g mozzarella or primo sole cheese, thinly sliced

100 g sliced salami or Parma ham, or whole anchovy fillets

a small bunch of fresh oregano or basil

sea salt and freshly ground black pepper

extra virgin olive oil, for drizzling

Serves 4

Preheat the oven to 220°C (425°F) Gas 7.

Heat the bread in the preheated oven for 5 minutes. While the bread is still hot, cut it in half lengthways and make small incisions all over the cut surfaces of both halves of the bread. Drizzle with olive oil and sprinkle with salt, pepper and half the oregano leaves. On the bottom half of the loaf, put a layer of tomato, followed by a layer of cheese. Top with the salami and the remaining oregano leaves. Sandwich the 2 halves together, wrap in aluminium foil and a clean tea towel, then transfer to a picnic basket.

Spain's celebrated thick tortilla omelette (*tortilla de patata*) is one of the world's most accommodating dishes. It's good for any occasion, particularly as a portable picnic food, but it's also very useful as a quick lunch dish eaten between slices of bread and even as a breakfast snack. Served with this scarlet piquillo sauce, it is delicious. In many Spanish bars and cafés, sliced courgettes, spinach, onion or red peppers may be added to the potatoes for variety, flavour and colour, but plain potato is the most common and well loved at home and abroad.

spanish potato omelette

100 ml extra virgin olive oil

1 kg salad potatoes, peeled and cut into 2 cm cubes

1 onion, sliced into rings

4 garlic cloves, finely chopped (optional)

6 eggs, beaten

4 tablespoons chopped fresh flat leaf parsley or spring onion tops

sea salt and freshly ground black pepper

Piquillo sauce

225 g tin or jar of roasted piquillo peppers or pimientos

3 tablespoons sherry vinegar

Serves 4–6

Heat the oil in a frying pan, add the potatoes and onion and cook over low heat for 12–14 minutes or until tender but not browned, moving them about with a fish slice so that they cook evenly. Add the garlic, if using, for the last 2 minutes.

Put the eggs, salt and pepper in a bowl and beat well.

Using a slotted spoon, remove the cooked potatoes and garlic from the pan and stir it into the egg mixture. Stir in the parsley.

Quickly pour the egg mixture back into the hot frying pan. Cook, not stirring, over low to moderate heat for 4–5 minutes or until firm, but do not let it brown too much. The top will still be wobbly and only partially cooked.

Holding a heatproof plate over the top of the omelette, quickly invert the pan, omelette and plate. Slide the hot omelette back, upside down, to brown the other side for 2–3 minutes more, then remove from the pan and leave to cool for 5 minutes.

To make the sauce, put the piquillo, 6 tablespoons of the liquid from the can (make it up with water if necessary) and the sherry vinegar in a blender. Purée to form a smooth, scarlet sauce.

Cut the omelette into chunks, segments or cubes. Serve the sauce separately, spooning some over the pieces of tortilla.

With its lovely, earthy flavours, a frittata is an Italian version of the Spanish tortilla or the French omelette, and different ingredients are added depending on the region or season. Eaten cold, it is ideal for a picnic.

mixed mushroom frittata

3 tablespoons extra virgin olive oil

2 shallots, finely chopped

2 garlic cloves, finely chopped

1 tablespoon chopped fresh thyme leaves

300 g mixed wild and cultivated mushrooms, such as girolle, chanterelle, portobello, shiitake and cep

6 eggs

2 tablespoons chopped fresh flat leaf parsley

sea salt and freshly ground black pepper

Serves 6

Put 2 tablespoons of the oil into a non-stick frying pan, heat gently, then add the shallots, garlic and thyme. Fry gently for 5 minutes until softened but not browned.

Meanwhile, brush off any dirt clinging to the mushrooms and wipe the caps. Chop or slice coarsely and add to the pan. Fry for 4–5 minutes until they just start to release their juices. Remove from the heat.

Put the eggs into a bowl with the parsley and a little salt and pepper, whisk briefly, then stir in the mushroom mixture. Wipe the frying pan clean. Preheat the grill.

Heat the remaining tablespoon of oil in the clean pan and pour in the egg and mushroom mixture. Cook over medium heat for 8–10 minutes until set on the bottom. Transfer to the preheated grill and cook for about 2–3 minutes until the top is set and spotted brown. Cool at room temperature before taking outdoors.

chilled avocado and pepper soup

A cold soup on a hot summer's day is difficult to beat. The secret is to make it look gorgeous while keeping the portions small. Glasses are a great idea for serving, showing off the vibrant green colour – utterly seductive.

1 tablespoon olive oil

1/2 onion, finely chopped

1 green pepper, deseeded and finely chopped

1/2 green chilli, deseeded and finely chopped

1 1/2 litres vegetable stock

freshly squeezed juice of 1 lime

1 avocado, halved and deseeded

a handful of fresh mint leaves

sea salt and freshly ground black pepper

Greek yoghurt, to serve

crushed ice, to serve

Serves 4

Put the oil, onion, green pepper and chilli in a saucepan and cook over gentle heat for about 20 minutes until completely soft. Leave to cool.

Transfer to a blender, add the vegetable stock, lime juice, avocado flesh and mint leaves, and purée until smooth. Add salt and pepper to taste, then serve in bowls or glasses, topped with a spoonful of yoghurt and some crushed ice.

This combination of salad leaves, all of them refreshing in taste and intense in colour, makes a cracking chilled summer soup. Plunging lightly cooked leaves and vegetables into iced water helps preserve their natural green pigment.

chilled spinach, rocket and watercress soup

4 shallots, chopped

2 garlic cloves, chopped

1/2 nutmeg, grated, plus extra to serve

100 ml white wine

400 ml vegetable stock

250 g mixed spinach, rocket and watercress leaves

200 ml single cream or yoghurt

sea salt and freshly ground black pepper

olive oil, for frying

4 teaspoons single cream, to serve

4 large leaves of wild rocket, to serve

Serves 4

Heat enough olive oil to cover the base of a frying pan, add the shallots, garlic and nutmeg and fry over low heat until the onions are soft. Add the wine and stock and bring to the boil, then simmer for 10 minutes. Remove from the heat and leave to cool.

Put the spinach, rocket and watercress in a large pan containing 1 litre of lightly salted boiling water, gently submerse the leaves with a spoon and blanch for 60 seconds. Drain and plunge the leaves into a bowl of cold water and ice to chill quickly. Drain and squeeze out the excess water with your hands.

Put the leaves and the soup in a food processor and blend to a smooth consistency. Add the cream and season with salt and pepper to taste. Cover and chill for at least 2 hours or overnight.

Ladle the soup into bowls, feather with cream and serve with rocket leaves and grated nutmeg.

Gazpacho is the famous iced tomato soup from Andalucia. This recipe calls for sweetly mellow Pedro Ximenez vinegar, produced from one of Spain's most distinguished sweet wines and available from good wine merchants, but if you can't find it, use sherry vinegar and sweet sherry instead. Serve the chilled soup with olive ice cubes in stemmed glasses on a small plate, as seen in tapas bars from Seville to Salvador. The flavour of the tomatoes is important. Green peppers, always included in Andalucia, are not everyone's favourite, so omit them if you prefer.

gazpacho pedro ximenez

To make decorative ice cubes, start the day before. Set 12 stuffed olives in an ice cube tray. Fill it with sparkling water and freeze. Keep until serving time.

Put the tomatoes, onion, cucumber, pepper, if using, and the tomato purée in a food processor or blender. Add the garlic, stale bread, half the vinegar, all the oil, and about 400 ml water. Purée the soup continuously until it becomes a smooth, brick-red mixture. Add salt and pepper to taste, then add the remaining vinegar. Blend again.

Pour into 4–6 stemmed glasses, each with 2–3 olive ice cubes. Set the remaining olives on the plate. Drink the soup straight from the glass: the olives act as additional seasoning.

Variations If you prefer, omit the olive-filled ice cubes and simply serve plain ice, with extra olives on the side.

To make croutons, cut an additional 1–1½ slices of stale bread into 1 cm cubes and fry in extra virgin olive oil until crisp. Serve with the soup for sprinkling on top.

250 g (about 2) ripe, red tomatoes, blanched, skinned and finely diced

½ red or white onion, finely chopped

100 g (about 20 cm) cucumber, peeled and finely diced

1 green pepper, deseeded and diced (optional)

1 tablespoon tomato purée

2 garlic cloves, chopped

60 g sliced stale bread, cubed

3 tablespoons Pedro Ximenez vinegar, or sherry vinegar plus 1 tablespoon sweet sherry

1 tablespoon extra virgin olive oil

sea salt and freshly ground black pepper

Green olive ice cubes

12 green Spanish olives, stuffed with anchovies or almonds

chilled sparkling water

Serves 4–6

salads

sweet glazed pepper salad

Don't think that there are too many peppers in this recipe – they will definitely all disappear!

10 red peppers, cut into large chunks and deseeded

5 red onions, quartered lengthways

4 tablespoons olive oil

5 tablespoons balsamic vinegar

2 tablespoons clear honey

400 g stoned kalamata or other black olives, chopped

sea salt and freshly ground black pepper

a sprig of parsley, to serve

Serves 20

Preheat the oven to 180°C (350°F) Gas 4.

Put the peppers and onions into a large bowl, add the olive oil and mix to coat. Transfer to 2 large roasting tins and cook in the preheated oven for 1 hour, turning the vegetables after 40 minutes so they will cook evenly. Add the vinegar, honey, olives, salt and pepper, mix well and set aside to cool.

Serve warm or cold, topped with a sprig of parsley.

summer salad

This quick and simple salad sparkles with the good, clean, peppery taste of watercress and the delicious crunch of radish and celery.

300 g watercress, ends trimmed

a bunch of radishes, trimmed and halved

6 celery stalks, sliced

4 tablespoons olive oil

2 tablespoons balsamic vinegar

sea salt and freshly ground black pepper

Serves 4

Put the watercress in a salad bowl, then add the halved radishes and sliced celery.

Drizzle with the olive oil. Add the vinegar and seasoning, toss well and enjoy.

Cook's tip Some salad items are not good travellers and by the time they make it from your shopping basket to the table, they may have seen better days. Replace any of the ingredients in the above salad with whatever is fresh and best in the market on the day: remember, shopping should always be flexible.

Pumpkin seeds and pumpkin seed oil seem to be back in fashion. Look for dark, sticky, roasted pumpkin seed oil in good delicatessens, and use it quickly because, once opened, it won't keep well. Alternatively, store in the coolest, darkest part of the refrigerator.

red leaf salad

2 small heads of radicchio (round shaped)

2 heads pointed red chicory (Belgian endive)

2 heads Italian-style pointed red escarole

1/4–1/2 head of red oakleaf lettuce

2 handfuls baby red chard leaves

1 tablespoon extra virgin olive oil

4 tablespoons husked pumpkin seeds

1 red onion, cut into fine segments or rings

Dressing

3 tablespoons extra virgin olive oil

4 tablespoons roasted pumpkin seed oil or extra virgin olive oil

1 tablespoon red wine or sherry vinegar

2 teaspoons Dijon mustard

1 tablespoon crème de cassis (optional)

sea salt and freshly ground black pepper

Serves 4

Wash the radicchio, chicory, escarole, lettuce and chard and separate into leaves. Dry well.

Put the 1 tablespoon olive oil in a frying pan, add the pumpkin seeds and toss over low heat until toasted and aromatic (take care because they can burn easily). Remove from the heat and leave to cool on a plate.

To make the dressing, put the olive and pumpkin seed oils in a salad bowl, add the vinegar, mustard, crème de cassis, if using, salt and pepper and beat with a fork until emulsified.

Add the leaves, red onion and pumpkin seeds, toss well, then serve.

This satisfying summer salad with a delicious hint of fresh mint makes a superb accompaniment to barbecued meat or fish.

courgette, feta and mint salad

Preheat the barbecue.

Put the sesame seeds into a dry frying pan and toast over medium heat until golden and aromatic. Remove from the heat, leave to cool and set aside until required.

Cut the courgettes diagonally into thick slices, toss with the olive oil and season with salt and pepper. Cook over hot coals for 2–3 minutes on each side until charred and tender. Remove and leave to cool.

Put all the dressing ingredients into a screw-top jar and shake well. Add salt and pepper to taste. Put the courgettes, feta and mint into a large bowl, add the dressing and toss well until evenly coated. Sprinkle with the sesame seeds and serve at once.

1 tablespoon sesame seeds

6 large courgettes

3 tablespoons extra virgin olive oil

150 g feta cheese, crumbled

a handful of fresh mint leaves

Dressing

4 tablespoons extra virgin olive oil

1 tablespoon freshly squeezed lemon juice

1 small garlic clove, crushed

sea salt and freshly ground black pepper

Serves 4

bean and mint salad

This mix of beans and fresh mint is very refreshing and clean on the palate, making it a great summer salad.

200 g broad beans, shelled and peeled

75 g peas, shelled

75 g dwarf or French beans, trimmed

75 g runner beans, sliced into 5 cm pieces

8 spring onions, trimmed and sliced

a large bunch of mint, coarsely chopped

3 tablespoons olive oil

grated zest and freshly squeezed juice of 1 unwaxed lemon

sea salt and freshly ground black pepper

Serves 4

Cook the broad beans in a large pan of boiling water for 4 minutes, then add the peas, dwarf or French beans and runner beans and continue cooking for 3 minutes. Drain, cool quickly under cold running water, then drain thoroughly.

Put the spring onions and mint in a large bowl. Add the beans, then sprinkle with the olive oil, lemon zest and juice, salt and pepper. Toss well and serve.

Cook's tip Turn this salad into a main course by adding crumbled feta cheese, sliced hard-boiled eggs or pieces of juicy roast ham.

leaf and herb salad

This may be a simple salad, but simplicity is best when you're working with the fragrant flavours of herbs. To make it extra pretty, garnish with edible flowers such as heartsease, nasturtiums and pansies, when available.

300 g mixed leaves or 1 head of lettuce

a handful of edible flowers (optional)

4 bunches of herbs, such as basil, chives, marjoram, flat leaf parsley, sage, tarragon, fennel and lovage

extra virgin olive oil, to drizzle

Serves 4

Wash and trim the mixed leaves or lettuce as necessary. Tear into a bowl. Add the edible flowers, if using, and a selection of your chosen herbs. Drizzle with olive oil, toss well and serve immediately.

For this Arab-influenced salad, try to use young, tender fennel bulbs and vividly juicy and colourful oranges (or try it with minneolas, clementines, satsumas or mandarins). To cut off all of the bitter pith, slice a piece off the top and base of each fruit, then slice off the skin and white pith from top to bottom using a fine, serrated vegetable knife, in a sawing movement – easy and effective. Orange flower water is sold in Italian and Middle Eastern shops.

fennel and orange salad

5 large unwaxed oranges, about 600 g, or equivalent weight of minneolas, clementines, satsumas or mandarins, washed and dried

1–2 heads of young fennel, preferably with green tops

2 red onions, thinly sliced

24 black olives, preferably the dry-cured Provençal type

Dressing

4 tablespoons extra virgin olive oil

1/2 teaspoon orange flower water or 1 tablespoon freshly squeezed orange juice or zest

1 teaspoon sea salt

1/2 teaspoon white, green or pink peppercorns, well crushed or chopped

Serves 4

Using a vegetable peeler, remove the zest of 1 orange or 2 smaller citrus fruits, then slice the zest into thin strips. Set aside. Halve and squeeze the juice from the zested fruit into a bowl.

Remove a slice from the top and bottom of the remaining fruit then prepare as described in the recipe introduction. Discard the debris. Slice each fruit crossways into thin rounds, adding any juice to the bowl.

Finely slice the fennel bulb lengthways. Toss it immediately in the bowl of juice. Assemble the fennel, oranges, onions and olives on a flat salad platter, then add the reserved zest and pour the juice over the top.

To make the dressing, put the olive oil, orange flower water, salt and pepper in a bowl or jar and beat or shake well. Pour the dressing over the salad and serve cool.

salade niçoise

2 garlic cloves, lightly crushed and halved

1 head of cos lettuce, or 1/2 head of Batavia or frisée

1 small gem lettuce or other crisp baby lettuce (optional)

2 spring onions, sliced

250–350 g good-quality tinned tuna pieces or cooked, cold, fresh tuna

50 g salted anchovies or 24 tinned salted anchovy fillets

24 black olives, Niçoise type (optional)

3 or 4 hard-boiled eggs, shelled and quartered or halved

a handful of fresh, small basil leaves, roughly torn

200 g fresh broad beans, podded and peeled

2 ripe red tomatoes, each cut into 6 or 8 wedges

10-cm piece of cucumber, peeled and cubed

2 fresh baby artichokes, trimmed, halved and chokes removed (or canned equivalent)

4 radishes, sliced

8 tablespoons extra virgin olive oil

1/2 teaspoon sea salt

1 lemon, cut into wedges (optional)

Serves 4–6

This is probably one of the world's best-known (but least well-made) salads. Debate rages over its provenance, but certain facts about its content seem immutable: anchovy fillets and tinned, good-quality tuna are vital, as are hard-boiled eggs. Also essential are tomatoes, cucumber, green pepper, onion, raw broad beans and basil leaves, while tender baby artichokes, ideally raw, are desirable. Black olives are optional, but usual. No cooked vegetables whatsoever are allowed, but if broad beans are unavailable, break the rules and substitute 150 g briefly cooked French beans. The garlic is best rubbed around the bowl, but it can also be crushed into the olive oil and lemon dressing poured over the salad. (However, many maintain that lemon is not permissible.) Think of this salad as a celebration of fresh flavours.

Rub the garlic cloves around the base and sides of each salad plate or bowl.

Wash and shake dry the salad leaves, then cover and chill. Tear them and use some of each type to line the plates or bowls. Scatter in some spring onions.

Break the tuna into coarse chunks and place on the lettuce. Rinse and dry the anchovies if very salty, then arrange in a criss-cross pattern on the tuna. Add the olives (if using), eggs and basil. Dot with the broad beans, tomatoes, cucumber, artichokes and radishes.

Whisk together the oil and the salt, adding the juice from 1 lemon wedge (if using). Drizzle this dressing over the salad just before serving, and put a wedge of lemon on each plate, if liked.

Pan bagnat
This dish, literally 'bathed bread' (from tomato juices and dressing), is essentially salade Niçoise packed into a large round boule or country loaf, the middle of which has been scooped out. It can also be made with lengths of hollowed-out baguette. The bread is pressed flat, wrapped in greaseproof paper, tied up and a weight placed on top. In 2–3 hours it is ready to unwrap and eat.

Cut pan bagnat looks gloriously colourful, like a layered terrine, and makes a splendid picnic dish.

kisir

This Turkish recipe is the perfect party salad. You can vary it depending on what you have available, substituting walnuts for hazelnuts or pistachios, for example, adding some olives or some finely snipped dried apricots or replacing the dill with fresh coriander.

250 g bulghur wheat

50 g roasted hazelnuts, chopped

50 g pistachio nuts, chopped

5–6 spring onions, trimmed and thinly sliced

1/2 cucumber, peeled, deseeded and finely chopped

1 red ramiro pepper, halved, deseeded and finely chopped

3 ripe tomatoes, skinned and finely chopped

1 pomegranate

freshly squeezed juice of 2 lemons

1/2 teaspoon salt

1 teaspoon ground cumin

1 teaspoon chilli flakes

3 tablespoons extra virgin olive oil

1 tablespoon pomegranate syrup or 2 teaspoons balsamic vinegar with 1 teaspoon sugar

5 tablespoons finely chopped parsley

3 tablespoons finely chopped mint leaves

3 tablespoons finely chopped dill

sea salt and freshly ground black pepper

Serves 8

Put the bulghur wheat in a large heatproof bowl and pour over enough boiling water to just cover the grain. Leave for 15 minutes for the liquid to absorb, then pour over plenty of cold water, swirl the grain around and tip into a sieve. Squeeze the grain with your hands to extract any excess water and return the grain to the bowl.

Add the nuts, spring onions, and cucumber, pepper and tomatoes (including the seeds and pulp). Halve the pomegranate and scoop out the seeds, reserving the juice and discarding the pith. Add the pomegranate seeds to the salad.

Whisk the lemon juice and reserved pomegranate juice with the salt, cumin and chilli flakes, whisk in the olive oil and pomegranate syrup and season with salt and pepper. Tip into the salad and mix well.

Finally, mix in the chopped herbs. Toss well together and check the seasoning, adding more salt, pepper or lemon juice to taste. Cover and set aside for at least an hour before serving for the flavours to infuse.

This dish, cooked on top of the stove, produces almost confit-style tomatoes; the more usual way is to oven-bake them. However, this homely method is very easy, especially for households without an oven, and luscious too.

Provençal tomatoes

6 medium ripe, flavourful tomatoes, halved horizontally

1 teaspoon sea salt

1 teaspoon caster sugar

8 black peppercorns

1/4 nutmeg, freshly grated

2 shallots, finely chopped

2 tablespoons extra virgin olive oil

2 garlic cloves, crushed or chopped

a handful of chopped mixed fresh herbs, such as chives, parsley, tarragon, borage, oregano and sage, or 2 teaspoons Provençal mixed dried herbs (if no fresh available)

3–4 tablespoons water or stock or white wine

3 tablespoons breadcrumbs, pan-sizzled in 1 tablespoon extra virgin olive oil

Serves 4

Scoop out and discard the seeds and juice from the tomatoes (or reserve for use another time).

Using a pestle and mortar, grind together the salt, sugar and peppercorns. Stir in the nutmeg. Sprinkle the tomatoes with this mixture, and put some shallots inside each one.

Heat the olive oil in a large, wide, heavy-based frying pan over high heat for 2 minutes. Add the tomatoes in a single layer, hollow side up. Scatter in the garlic and half the herbs, then cook for 2 minutes on a fairly high heat, uncovered.

Add 2 tablespoons of the water, stock or wine. Cover the pan, reduce the heat to its lowest setting and cook for 10 minutes more.

Use a spoon and palette knife to turn the tomatoes, being careful to keep neat shapes. If there is no liquid left, add 2 more tablespoons of the water, stock or wine. Cover the pan again and continue cooking for 10 minutes more. By now the tomatoes should be sticky, nearly collapsed and very fragrant.

Serve them right side up, with any of the sticky reside from the pan, and sprinkled with the remaining fresh herbs and a few toasted breadcrumbs, if liked. Enjoy hot, warm or cool.

camargue rice salad

Inspired by the cuisine of Camargue in southern Provence, this rice salad is excellent served warm, cool or cold.

50 g salted butter

2 red onions, sliced

200 g Camargue red rice, washed and drained

100 g Camargue or other long-grain white rice, washed and drained

1 fresh bouquet garni of thyme, sage, bay and oregano

2 dried chillies, crushed but whole

finely grated zest and freshly squeezed juice of 1 orange

finely grated zest and freshly squeezed juice of 1 unwaxed lemon

1¹/₂ teaspoons sea salt

50 g baby capers

50 g green or black olives

2 tablespoons concentrated chicken bouillon or 1 stock cube, crumbled

Serves 4–6

Heat a heavy-based flameproof casserole and melt the butter. Fry the red onions over high heat for 2 minutes.

In a separate pan, bring 400 ml of water to the boil, add the red rice and return to the boil. Reduce the heat to a simmer, cover the pan and cook for 25–30 minutes, or until the rice is al dente.

Scatter the white rice and all the remaining ingredients (reserving a little zest) into the pan with the onions. Add 200 ml boiling water.

Return to the boil, then simmer, covered, for 10–12 minutes, or until the rice is tender and all the liquid has been absorbed. Remove the bouquet garni and chillies. Stir in the cooked red rice.

To serve, pile up the rice, scatter with the reserved citrus zests and eat as a warm salad. Alternatively, serve cool or cold.

broad bean salad
with mint and parmesan

This salad, served with a hazelnut oil dressing, makes a wonderful addition to a picnic spread. If it's early in the season and you have young, tender broad beans, it's not necessary to peel them after blanching. Out of season, you can use frozen broad beans or flat beans cut into 3 cm lengths.

750 g podded, young fresh or frozen broad beans

3 heads of chicory

leaves from 3 sprigs of mint

25 g Parmesan cheese

Dressing

2 tablespoons extra virgin olive oil

4 tablespoons hazelnut oil*

2 teaspoons white wine vinegar

1 teaspoon Dijon mustard

1/4 teaspoon sugar

sea salt and freshly ground black pepper

Serves 6

Plunge the broad beans into a saucepan of lightly salted, boiling water, return to the boil and simmer for 1–2 minutes. Drain and refresh the beans immediately under cold running water. Pat dry and peel away the grey-green outer skin if necessary. Put the peeled beans into a salad bowl.

Cut the chicory in half lengthways, slice thickly crossways, then add to the beans. Add the mint leaves, tearing any large ones in half. Using a potato peeler, cut thin shavings of Parmesan over the salad.

Just before serving, put the dressing ingredients into a small jug, mix well, sprinkle over the salad, toss well, then serve.

* If hazelnut oil is difficult to find, substitute extra virgin olive oil. Always buy nut oils in small quantities and keep them in the refrigerator: they are delicate, and become rancid very quickly.

Fresh mozzarella is essential for this recipe. Made from cow's or buffalo's milk, these soft white balls of cheese are best enjoyed within a day or two of being made. This fresh cheese is quite different from the firmer yellow mozzarella frequently used on pizza and lasagne.

mozzarella, peach and frisée salad

3 fresh peaches, cut into thin wedges

4 handfuls of frisée leaves, trimmed

1 large ball of buffalo mozzarella, torn into thin shreds

3 tablespoons extra virgin olive oil

1 tablespoon white wine vinegar

freshly ground black pepper

Serves 4

Put the peach wedges and frisée in a large bowl and gently toss to mix. Arrange on a serving plate. Scatter the mozzarella pieces over the salad.

Put the olive oil, vinegar and black pepper in a bowl, whisk with a fork, and then spoon over the salad to serve.

Variations Replace the mozzarella with 150 g crumbled firm blue cheese and the frisée with spinach leaves. Alternatively, keep the mozzarella and replace the other ingredients with fresh slices of tomato, basil leaves and some fruity extra virgin olive oil.

Orzo is a rice-shaped pasta, ideal for making into a salad because it retains its shape and texture after cooking.

orzo salad
with lemon and herb dressing

250 g cherry tomatoes, halved

6 tablespoons extra virgin olive oil

250 g orzo or other tiny soup pasta*

6 spring onions, finely chopped

4 tablespoons coarsely chopped mixed fresh herbs, such as basil, dill, mint and parsley

grated zest and freshly squeezed juice of 2 unwaxed lemons

sea salt and freshly ground black pepper

4 wooden skewers, soaked in water for 30 minutes

Serves 4

Preheat the barbecue or grill.

Thread the tomatoes onto the soaked wooden skewers with all the cut halves facing the same way. Sprinkle with a little olive oil, season with salt and pepper and cook over hot coals or under the grill for 1–2 minutes on each side until lightly charred and softened. Remove from the heat and set aside.

Bring a large saucepan of lightly salted water to the boil. Add the orzo and cook for about 9 minutes or until al dente. Drain well and transfer to a large bowl.

Heat 2 tablespoons of the olive oil in a frying pan, add the onions, herbs and lemon zest and stir-fry for 30 seconds. Stir into the orzo, then add the tomatoes, lemon juice, remaining olive oil, salt and pepper. Toss well and leave to cool before serving.

* If orzo is unavailable, use other pasta shapes instead.

pasta, squash and feta salad
with olive dressing

Tapenade is an essential ingredient of the olive dressing. You can buy this paste ready-made but by far the best tapenade is the one you make yourself (see page 12).

750 g butternut squash

1 tablespoon extra virgin olive oil

1 tablespoon chopped fresh thyme leaves

500 g dried penne

350 g feta cheese, diced

350 g cherry tomatoes, halved

4 tablespoons chopped fresh basil

4 tablespoons pumpkin seeds, toasted in a dry frying pan

sea salt and freshly ground black pepper

Dressing

150 ml extra virgin olive oil

3 tablespoons Tapenade (page 12)

freshly squeezed juice of 1 lemon

1 teaspoon clear honey

sea salt and freshly ground black pepper

Serves 6

Preheat the oven to 200°C (400°F) Gas 6.

Peel and deseed the butternut squash and cut the flesh into bite-sized pieces. Put into a bowl or plastic bag, then add the oil, thyme, salt and pepper. Toss well, then arrange in a single layer in a roasting tin. Roast in the preheated oven for about 25 minutes until golden and tender. Leave to cool.

To make the dressing, put the olive oil, tapenade, lemon juice and honey into a bowl. Whisk well, then add salt and pepper to taste.

Bring a large saucepan of lightly salted water to the boil, add the penne and cook for about 10 minutes until al dente. Drain well, then stir in 4 tablespoons of the dressing. Leave to cool.

When cool, put the pasta and squash into a salad bowl, mix gently, then add the feta cheese, cherry tomatoes, basil and toasted pumpkin seeds. Just before serving, stir in the remaining dressing.

lobster salad
with chilli dressing

Ready-cooked and halved lobsters are easy to find, and some people may prefer to buy them like this rather than prepare them from scratch. But, if you have time and want to cook them yourself, it's well worth the effort because you can guarantee that the lobster will be really fresh. If lobsters are difficult to get hold of, or too expensive, try substituting monkfish, often called 'poor man's lobster', or even boneless chicken breasts, tossed in olive oil, then roasted in a hot oven for about 25 minutes. Deseed the chillies in the chilli dressing only if you are fearful of heat.

8 small or 4 large lobsters

650 g potatoes, cut into chunks

a bunch of fresh coriander, coarsely chopped

1 red onion, very thinly sliced

sea salt and freshly ground black pepper

leafy salad, to serve

Dressing

1 green or red chilli, deseeded (optional) and chopped

5 cm fresh ginger, peeled and chopped

5 garlic cloves, crushed

2 tablespoons white wine vinegar

6 tablespoons caster sugar

Serves 8

To make the dressing, put the chilli, ginger and garlic into a saucepan. Add the vinegar and sugar and simmer over low heat, stirring frequently, for 10 minutes, until reduced by half. Add 2 tablespoons water, remove from the heat and leave to cool.

If cooking the lobsters live, bring a large saucepan of water to the boil. Plunge the lobsters carefully into the boiling water, cover with a lid and simmer for 10 minutes per 500 g. Drain and leave to cool.

When cool, remove the claws and legs. Using a large, sharp knife, split each body in half lengthways, holding the lobster with a tea towel in your other hand to stop it slipping. Crack open the claws and remove the flesh, leaving it in whole pieces. Remove the flesh from the split body halves and cut into thick slices. Reserve the shells.

Cook the potatoes in a saucepan of boiling, salted water for 20 minutes, until tender when pierced with a knife. Drain and leave to cool. Add the coriander and chopped lobster to the potatoes, with salt and pepper to taste. Mix lightly, then spoon the mixture into the empty lobster shells, piling it in generously. Spoon over the dressing, sprinkle with the onion slices and serve with a leafy salad.

If you've never eaten a Japanese salad, this will be a delightful surprise. The salad itself is a simple combination of fresh ingredients plus two types of Japanese noodles – but it's the dressing that makes this so interesting.

japanese garden salad
with noodles

100 g soba noodles

100 g udon noodles

250 g mangetout

2 cos lettuce hearts or Little Gem lettuces, leaves separated

2 carrots

1 cucumber

4 ripe tomatoes

Dressing

2 tablespoons Japanese soy sauce (shoyu)

1 1/2 tablespoons sugar

1 1/2 tablespoons rice vinegar

1 tablespoon sesame oil

Serves 6

Cook the noodles separately according to the instructions on the packet. Drain and set aside.

Blanch the mangetout in lightly salted, boiling water for 1 minute. Drain, refresh under cold water and dry well.

Wash and dry the lettuce leaves. Cut the carrot and cucumber into matchsticks and the tomatoes into wedges. Divide the noodles and salad ingredients between 6 serving bowls.

Put the dressing ingredients into a bowl, add 150 ml water and stir well until the sugar has dissolved. Pour over the salad and serve at once.

Asparagus in season is pure delight. Add the delicate sweetness of Parma ham, dried to crispness, and you have an unusual combination. Use white asparagus if you can find it (French and Italian greengrocers often stock this during early summer), though green asparagus is more usual. This dish goes particularly well served with *frizzante*, such as Lambrusco, or a crisp, dry, white wine.

asparagus with prosciutto

8 thin slices (about 150–200 g) prosciutto, such as Parma ham

500 g bunch of thick asparagus

2 tablespoons extra virgin olive oil or lemon oil

Serves 4

Before turning on the oven, hang the slices of prosciutto over the grids of the top oven rack. Slide the rack into the oven, then turn it on to 150°C (300°F) Gas 2. Leave for 20 minutes until the ham is dry and crisp. Remove carefully and set aside.

Preheat the grill. Using a vegetable peeler, peel 7 cm of the tough skin off the end of each asparagus spear, then snap off and discard any tough ends. Arrange the asparagus in a shallow baking tray and sprinkle with the oil. Cook under the preheated grill for 6–8 minutes, or until the asparagus is wrinkled and tender.

Serve the asparagus with some of the hot oil from the grill pan and 2 prosciutto 'crisps' for each person.

ham and melon platter

For colour contrast you need an orange Canteloupe or Charentais melon and a green Galia, Ogen or Honeydew melon, and some thinly sliced Parma ham and *prosciutto cotto all'erbe*. Quarter and deseed the melons, cut the wedges off the skin, then cut them into thick slices. Arrange on a big plate along with loosely draped slices of ham. The platter wants to look quite casual – lavish and generous, rather than arranged into perfectly lined up rows.

Serve the platter with some olive breadsticks and mini ciabattas, refreshed in the oven.

chicken salad
with radicchio and pine nuts

This salad is delightful, with the rich, almost plum-like flavours of its Marsala raisin dressing. If you can't find sherry vinegar, one of the most delicious vinegars, use balsamic instead.

1 small red onion, sliced

750 g cooked chicken breast

1 head of radicchio, shredded

125 g rocket leaves

a few sprigs of flat leaf parsley

Dressing

100 ml extra virgin olive oil

50 g pine nuts

75 g raisins

2 tablespoons Marsala wine

2 tablespoons sherry vinegar

sea salt and freshly ground black pepper

Serves 4–6

Put the onion slices into a small bowl and cover with cold water. Leave to soak for 30 minutes, drain well, then dry thoroughly with kitchen paper.

Tear or slice the chicken into thin strips and put into a large salad bowl. Add the radicchio, rocket leaves, parsley and onion.

To make the dressing, put 2 tablespoons of the oil into a frying pan, heat gently, add the pine nuts and raisins and fry for 3–4 minutes until the pine nuts are lightly golden. Add the Marsala and vinegar, with salt and pepper to taste, and leave to warm through. Stir in the remaining oil and remove from the heat.

Pour the dressing over the salad, toss lightly and serve.

turmeric lamb fillet
with couscous salad

There are two cuts of lamb fillet that can be used for this dish. One is from the eye of the cutlets and truly melt-in-the-mouth but expensive. The other, from the neck, is more marbled with fat but far cheaper.

Preheat the barbecue.

Put the turmeric, cinnamon, curry powder, garlic, oil and honey into a bowl, add salt and pepper to taste and stir well. Trim any excess fat off the lamb fillets and rub the spice mixture all over. Transfer to a dish, cover and chill overnight.

To make the couscous salad, put the couscous and saffron into a large bowl. Pour over 400 ml boiling water, mix and set aside for 15 minutes until all the liquid has been absorbed.

Meanwhile, heat the butter and oil in a large frying pan, add the onions and cook for 8 minutes until golden and slightly frizzled. Add the garlic and cook for a further 2 minutes, then add the onions and garlic to the prepared couscous.

Add the pistachio nuts, lemon zest and juice, coriander and salt and pepper to taste, mix well and set aside.

Cook the lamb fillets on the hot barbecue for about 25 minutes for medium rare, turning them frequently and basting with any extra marinade. Remove to a board, slice and serve with the couscous salad.

Turmeric lamb

3 teaspoons ground turmeric

1 teaspoon ground cinnamon

3 teaspoons medium curry powder

2 garlic cloves, chopped

3 tablespoons olive oil

4 tablespoons clear honey

1.5 kg lamb fillets

sea salt and freshly ground black pepper

Couscous salad

375 g couscous

1/2 teaspoon saffron threads

25 g unsalted butter

2 tablespoons olive oil

4 onions, sliced

1 garlic clove, chopped

100 g shelled pistachio nuts, coarsely chopped

grated zest and freshly squeezed juice of 2 unwaxed lemons

a large bunch of fresh coriander, chopped

sea salt and freshly ground black pepper

Serves 8

figs with crispy prosciutto, blue cheese and rocket

The flavours in this salad are so simple and classic, and here's the trick: get your hands on the best produce and all the hard work is done already! Have the prosciutto sliced fresh from the leg at the deli and you will notice the difference. You don't have to cook the prosciutto to a crisp if you prefer not to, although the crispy texture does go very well with sweet honey-flavoured figs, in the same way that crispy bacon goes so well with maple syrup.

3 tablespoons light olive oil

6 thin slices of prosciutto, such as Parma ham

2 tablespoons red wine vinegar

1 teaspoon Dijon mustard

80–100 g wild rocket

6 figs, quartered

150 g firm blue cheese (such as Wensleydale or Yorkshire Blue), crumbled

sea salt and freshly ground black pepper

Serves 4

Heat the olive oil in a non-stick frying pan over medium heat and cook the prosciutto for 1 minute on each side, until crispy, and place on kitchen paper. When cool enough to handle, break the prosciutto into smaller pieces. Pour the oil from the pan into a small bowl and add the vinegar, mustard, a pinch of sea salt and freshly ground black pepper to taste.

Arrange the rocket on a serving plate with the fig quarters on top. Scatter over the cheese and the prosciutto pieces. Pour the dressing evenly over the salad when ready to serve.

thai-style beef salad

Many Thai salads, as well as soups and stews, are flooded with the pungent flavours of fresh herbs, in particular Thai basil, mint and coriander. Thai basil is available from Asian grocers, but if you can't get hold of any, you could use the ordinary variety instead. Pak-choi is also known as bok choy.

1 tablespoon Szechuan peppercorns, or black peppercorns, lightly crushed

1 teaspoon ground coriander

1 teaspoon sea salt

500 g beef fillet, in the piece

1 tablespoon peanut or vegetable oil

1 cucumber, thinly sliced

4 spring onions, thinly sliced

2 baby pak-choi, thinly sliced

a handful of fresh Thai basil

a handful of fresh mint

a handful of fresh coriander leaves

Dressing

15 g palm sugar or brown sugar

1 tablespoon Thai fish sauce

2 tablespoons freshly squeezed lime juice

2 red chillies, deseeded and chopped

1 garlic clove, crushed

Serves 4

Preheat the barbecue.

Put the peppercorns, ground coriander and salt onto a plate and mix. Rub the beef all over with the oil and then put onto the plate and turn to coat with the spices.

Cook the beef on the preheated barbecue or a ridged stove-top grill pan for about 10 minutes, turning to brown evenly. Remove from the heat and leave to cool.

Meanwhile, to make the dressing, put the sugar into a saucepan, add the fish sauce and 2 tablespoons water and heat until the sugar dissolves. Leave to cool, then stir in the lime juice, chillies and garlic.

Cut the beef into thin slices and put into a large bowl. Add the cucumber, spring onions, pak-choi and herbs. Pour over the dressing, toss well, then serve.

barbecues

The nut sauce, tarator, served with these leeks is found in Middle Eastern cooking, although it would traditionally be made with ground almonds or walnuts instead of toasted macadamias. The sauce can be made in advance, but make sure that you whisk it well before using.

charred leeks
with tarator sauce

750 g baby leeks, trimmed

2–3 tablespoons extra virgin olive oil

sea salt

a few lemon wedges, to serve

Tarator sauce

50 g macadamia nuts, toasted

25 g fresh breadcrumbs

2 garlic cloves, crushed

100 ml extra virgin olive oil

1 tablespoon freshly squeezed lemon juice

sea salt and freshly ground black pepper

Serves 4

Preheat the barbecue.

To make the sauce, put the nuts into a food processor and grind coarsely, then add the breadcrumbs, garlic, salt and pepper. Process again to form a smooth paste. Transfer to a bowl and very gradually whisk in the olive oil, lemon juice and 2 tablespoons boiling water to form a sauce. Season to taste with salt and pepper.

Brush the leeks with a little olive oil, season with salt and cook on the barbecue over medium-hot coals for 6–10 minutes, turning occasionally, until charred and tender.

Transfer to a serving plate, sprinkle with olive oil, then pour the sauce over the top and serve with the lemon wedges.

barbecued
courgettes

8 courgettes, cut lengthways into 1 cm slices

olive oil

balsamic vinegar

sea salt and freshly ground black pepper

Serves 8

Preheat the barbecue. Cook the courgette slices over medium heat for 3–4 minutes on each side, until lightly charred. Remove to a plate and sprinkle with oil, vinegar, salt and pepper. Serve hot, warm or cold.

chargrilled dill polenta
with lemon, fennel and spring onions

Polenta provides a good base for the flavours of this barbecue dish. There are three ingredients that fennel should possibly never be without: lemon, olive oil and dill. Don't worry if you don't have any fresh dill – chop up the feathery fronds from the top of the fennel and use them instead.

30 g unsalted butter

1 tablespoon olive oil

200 g instant polenta

30 g Parmesan cheese, grated, plus extra to serve

20 g fresh dill, coarsely chopped

grated zest of ½ unwaxed lemon

sea salt and freshly ground black pepper

Marinated fennel

2 tablespoons sherry or red wine vinegar

3 tablespoons olive oil

2 garlic cloves, crushed

2 bulbs of fennel, tough outer leaves removed, remainder sliced

sea salt and freshly ground black pepper

Marinated spring onions

8 spring onions

1 tablespoon sherry or red wine vinegar

1 tablespoon olive oil

sea salt and freshly ground black pepper

a Swiss roll tin, 33 x 23 cm, lightly greased

a biscuit cutter, 9 cm diameter

Serves 4

To make the polenta, melt the butter and olive oil in a saucepan. Add 1.25 litres water and bring to the boil. Pour in the polenta in a steady stream, whisking all the time. Continue to cook, according to the instructions on the packet, until the grainy texture has disappeared. Stir in the Parmesan, dill, salt and pepper. Spoon into the prepared Swiss roll tin, then leave to cool until firm.

To marinate the fennel, put the vinegar, olive oil, garlic, salt and pepper in a bowl and mix well. Add the fennel and set aside to develop the flavours.

To marinate the spring onions, put the spring onions, vinegar, olive oil, salt and pepper in a separate bowl and set aside.

Preheat the barbecue.

Cut out rounds of polenta with the biscuit cutter. Cook on the preheated barbecue for 5 minutes on each side, until browned.

Add the fennel to the barbecue. Cook for 5–10 minutes until charred on both sides and tender. While the fennel is cooking, add the spring onions and cook for 2–3 minutes until lightly blackened.

Serve the polenta piled high with fennel and spring onions and sprinkle with Parmesan, lemon zest and sea salt. Pour any remaining marinade juices over the top.

tofu
in a hot, sweet and spicy infusion

Tofu receives some bad press and it can be exceedingly dull and tasteless when served au naturel. However, it does act as a sponge for marinades. The flavours of a marinade percolate all the way through, giving the tofu a fantastic extra lease of life and great versatility. For vegetarians, it is an excellent source of protein and, for meat-eaters, a welcome fat-free alternative.

Bury foil-wrapped potatoes in the embers of a bonfire on Guy Fawkes Night and then enjoy jacket potatoes cooked to perfection – a crispy skin with soft, fluffy insides – by the time the fireworks are over.

ember-roasted potatoes

4 medium roasting potatoes, such as King Edward or Desirée

salted butter, to serve

sea salt and freshly ground black pepper

Serves 4

Wrap the potatoes individually in a double layer of foil and, as soon as the coals are glowing red, put the potatoes on top. Rake the charcoal up and around them, but without covering them. Leave to cook for about 25 minutes, then using tongs, turn the potatoes over carefully and cook for a further 25–30 minutes until cooked through.

Remove from the heat and carefully remove the foil, then cut the potatoes in half. Serve, topped with a spoonful of butter, salt and pepper.

Variation For ember-roasted sweet potatoes, follow the same method but cook for about 20 minutes on each side.

250 g firm tofu

2 tablespoons hoisin sauce

3 tablespoons soy sauce

1 red chilli, finely chopped

2 cm fresh ginger, peeled and grated

1 teaspoon sesame oil

1 tablespoon rice vinegar

a handful of fresh coriander, coarsely chopped, to serve

Serves 4

Cut through the cake of tofu horizontally to make 2 thin slices. Cut each slice into 4 pieces.

Put the hoisin, soy sauce, chilli, ginger, sesame oil and rice vinegar in a small bowl and mix well. Pour onto a large plate, then put the tofu on top. Spoon some of the mixture over the top so that the tofu is completely covered. Leave for as long as possible to soak up the flavours, at least 2 hours or overnight.

Preheat the barbecue.

Put the tofu on the preheated barbecue, reserving some of the marinade. Barbecue each side for 4–5 minutes until lightly browned. Serve immediately with the reserved marinade, topped with coriander.

aubergine and smoked cheese rolls

Truly at home in both Middle Eastern and Mediterranean cuisines, aubergines are compatible with endless spices, herbs and a multitude of other ingredients. In this dish, they soak up the fragrance of spices and are paired with smoked cheese, enhancing the already smoky barbecue flavour.

Arrange the aubergine slices on a large tray. Mix the chilli and olive oils, cumin, garlic, chilli, mint, salt and pepper in a measuring jug, then pour over the aubergines. Turn each slice over so that both sides are well coated. Cover with clingfilm and set aside for a few hours or overnight to soak up all the flavours.

Preheat the barbecue.

Put the aubergines on the preheated barbecue. Barbecue for about 4 minutes, then turn and barbecue the other side until tender and browned.

Remove from the heat, put some of the cheese at one end of a slice of aubergine and roll up firmly (do this while the aubergine is still hot so the cheese melts). Repeat with the other slices. Sprinkle with the coriander and lemon juice, then serve.

2 aubergines, cut lengthways into about 5 slices

1 teaspoon chilli oil

125 ml olive oil

3 teaspoons cumin seeds, lightly toasted in a dry frying pan and ground

2 garlic cloves, crushed

1 red chilli, deseeded and finely chopped

a large handful of fresh mint leaves, finely chopped

175 g firm smoked cheese, sliced

sea salt and freshly ground black pepper

a large handful of fresh coriander, coarsely chopped, to serve

freshly squeezed juice of 1/2 lemon, to serve

Makes 10 rolls

Fatoush is a salad made with grilled pita bread. It's often served with halloumi, a firm cheese that can be chargrilled. Here is a version made with fresh mozzarella which can also be cooked on a barbecue, picking up an appealing smokiness in the process.

grilled pita salad
with olive salsa and mozzarella

250 g fresh mozzarella cheese, drained

1 large green pepper, deseeded and chopped

1 mini cucumber, chopped

2 ripe tomatoes, chopped

1/2 red onion, finely chopped

2 pita breads

4 tablespoons extra virgin olive oil

freshly squeezed juice of 1/2 lemon

sea salt and freshly ground black pepper

Olive salsa

75 g Kalamata olives, stoned and chopped

1 tablespoon chopped fresh parsley

1 small garlic clove, finely chopped

4 tablespoons extra virgin olive oil

1 tablespoon freshly squeezed lemon juice

freshly ground black pepper

Serves 4

Preheat the barbecue. Squeeze the mozzarella to remove excess water, then cut into thick slices. Brush the slices well with olive oil. Cook over the hot coals for 1 minute on each side until the cheese is charred with lines and beginning to soften. Alternatively, simply slice the cheese and use without grilling.

Put the green pepper, cucumber, tomatoes and onion into a bowl. Toast the pita breads over hot coals, cool slightly, then tear into bite-sized pieces. Add to the bowl, then pour over the olive oil and lemon juice. Season and stir well.

Put all the ingredients for the olive salsa into a bowl and stir well.

Spoon the salad onto small plates, top with a few slices of mozzarella and some olive salsa, then serve.

For this dish, you need beetroot and baby onions of roughly the same size, so they will barbecue evenly. It is an excellent accompaniment to grilled meats or salads.

beetroot and baby onion brochettes

32 large fresh bay leaves

20 small beetroot

20 baby onions, unpeeled

3 tablespoons extra virgin olive oil

1 tablespoon balsamic vinegar

sea salt and freshly ground black pepper

8 metal skewers

Serves 4

Put the bay leaves into a bowl, cover with cold water and leave to soak for 1 hour.

Cut the stalks off the beetroot and wash well under cold running water. Put the beetroot and baby onions into a large saucepan of lightly salted boiling water and blanch for 5 minutes. Drain and refresh under cold running water. Pat dry with kitchen paper, then peel the onions.

Preheat the barbecue.

Thread the beetroot, onions and damp bay leaves onto the skewers, sprinkle with the olive oil and vinegar and season well with salt and pepper. Barbecue over medium-hot coals for 20–25 minutes, turning occasionally, until charred and tender, then serve.

This is just the ticket for those who don't eat meat but love a good burger. The onion jam can be made in advance and kept in the refrigerator for several days.

mushroom burgers
with onion jam

To make the onion jam, heat the olive oil in a saucepan, add the onions and fry gently for 15 minutes or until very soft. Add a pinch of salt, the redcurrant jelly, vinegar and 2 tablespoons water and cook for a further 15 minutes or until the mixture is glossy with a jam-like consistency. Remove from the heat and leave to cool.

Preheat the barbecue.

Brush the olive oil over the mushrooms, season well with salt and pepper and barbecue, stem side down, for 5 minutes. Flip and barbecue for a further 5 minutes until the mushrooms are tender.

Toast the burger bun halves for a few moments on the barbecue and fill with the mushrooms, salad leaves, onion jam and a spoonful of mayonnaise.

2 tablespoons extra virgin olive oil

4 large portobello mushrooms, trimmed

4 burger buns, split in half

salad leaves

mayonnaise, to serve

sea salt and freshly ground black pepper

Onion jam

2 tablespoons olive oil

2 red onions, thinly sliced

4 tablespoons redcurrant jelly

1 tablespoon red wine vinegar

Serves 4

20 uncooked tiger prawns

250 g fillet steak

dipping sauces, to serve

Prawn marinade

1 teaspoon coriander seeds

1/2 teaspoon cumin seeds

1 garlic clove, crushed

1 teaspoon peeled and grated fresh ginger

2 kaffir lime leaves, shredded

1 teaspoon ground turmeric

1 tablespoon light soy sauce

4 tablespoons coconut milk

1/2 teaspoon salt

Beef marinade

1 garlic clove, crushed

2 stalks of lemongrass, trimmed and finely chopped

1 tablespoon peeled and grated fresh ginger

4 coriander roots, finely chopped

1 red chilli, finely chopped

grated zest and freshly squeezed juice of 1 unwaxed lime

1 tablespoon Thai fish sauce

1 tablespoon dark soy sauce

1 1/2 tablespoons sugar

1 tablespoon sesame oil

freshly ground black pepper

40 wooden skewers, soaked in water for 30 minutes

Serves 4

Satays are found all over South-east Asia. They are very easy to make and taste simply wonderful.

prawn and beef satays

Shell and devein the prawns, wash them under cold running water and pat dry with kitchen paper. Put them into a shallow dish.

To make the prawn marinade, put the coriander and cumin seeds into a dry frying pan and toast over medium heat until golden and aromatic. Remove, leave to cool slightly, then transfer to a spice grinder. Add the garlic, ginger and lime leaves and grind to a coarse paste. Alternatively, use a mortar and pestle.

Transfer to a bowl, add the turmeric, soy sauce, coconut milk and salt and mix well. Pour over the prawns and leave to marinate in the refrigerator for 1 hour.

To make the beef satays, cut the fillet steak across the grain into thin strips. Mix all the beef marinade ingredients in a shallow dish, add the beef strips and leave to marinate for about 1 hour.

Preheat the barbecue.

To assemble the beef satays, thread the beef strips onto the skewers, zig-zagging back and forth as you go. To assemble the prawn satays, thread the prawns lengthways onto the skewers.

Barbecue both kinds of satays over hot coals for 2 minutes each side, brushing the beef marinade over the beef satays halfway through. Serve hot with your choice of dipping sauces.

Piri-piri, a Portuguese chilli condiment traditionally used to baste grilled chicken, is a combination of chopped red chillies, olive oil and vinegar. It is generally very hot and only a drizzle is needed to add spice to grilled food. The sauce in this recipe is not particularly hot, but you can use more chillies if you like it hotter. It works very well with squid.

squid piri-piri

To prepare the squid, put the squid tube on a board and, using a sharp knife, cut down one side and open the tube out flat. Scrape away any remaining insides and wash and dry well.

Skewer each opened-out tube with 2 skewers, running them up the long sides of each piece. Rub a little sea salt over each one and squeeze over the lemon juice. Marinate in the refrigerator for 30 minutes.

Meanwhile, to make the piri-piri, finely chop the whole chillies without deseeding them and transfer to a small jar or bottle. Add the oil, vinegar and a little salt and pepper. Shake well and set aside.

Preheat the barbecue until hot.

Baste the squid with a little of the piri-piri and barbecue for 1–1½ minutes on each side until charred. Drizzle with extra sauce and serve with lemon wedges.

* If the squid includes the tentacles, cut them off in one piece, thread with a skewer and cook and marinate in the same way as the tubes.

8 medium squid tubes, about 250 g each*

freshly squeezed juice of 1 lemon, plus extra lemon wedges, to serve

sea salt

Piri-piri sauce

8 small red chillies

300 ml extra virgin olive oil

1 tablespoon white wine vinegar

sea salt and freshly ground black pepper

16 wooden skewers, soaked in water for 30 minutes

Serves 4

Meat and fish (the old-fashioned surf 'n' turf) can work well and this recipe is a perfect example of this balance of strong flavours. Here, chorizo sausage that needs cooking has been used, rather than the cured tapas variety, but either would do.

prawn, chorizo and sage skewers

300 g uncooked chorizo

24 uncooked shelled tiger prawns, deveined

24 large fresh sage leaves

extra virgin olive oil

a squeeze of fresh lemon juice

freshly ground black pepper

12 wooden skewers, soaked in water for 30 minutes

Serves 6

Cut the chorizo into 24 slices about 1 cm thick and thread onto the skewers, alternating with the prawns and sage leaves. Put a little olive oil and lemon juice into a small bowl or jug, mix well, then drizzle over the skewers. Sprinkle with pepper.

Preheat the barbecue until hot.

Barbecue the skewers for 1½–2 minutes on each side until the chorizo and prawns are cooked through. Serve at once.

2 spicy uncooked chorizo sausages

20 freshly shucked oysters

Shallot vinegar

3 tablespoons red wine vinegar

2 tablespoons finely chopped shallots

1 tablespoon snipped fresh chives

sea salt and freshly ground black pepper

cocktail sticks

a large platter filled with a layer of ice cubes

Serves 4

This combination may sound slightly unusual, but it is, in fact, totally delicious. Fresh oysters, a nibble of the hot sausages and a sip of chilled white wine is a taste sensation – try it, you'll be amazed.

oysters with spicy chorizo

To make the shallot vinegar, put the ingredients into a bowl and mix well. Pour into a small dish and set aside until required.

Preheat the barbecue.

Barbecue the sausages over hot coals for 8–10 minutes or until cooked through. Cut the sausages into bite-sized pieces and spike them onto cocktail sticks. Arrange in the centre of a large serving platter filled with ice. Put the oysters into their half-shells and arrange on the ice. Serve with the shallot vinegar.

Chunks of swordfish coated in a spicy rub, then barbecued on skewers and served with freshly cooked couscous, make the perfect alfresco lunch.

moroccan fish skewers
with couscous

750 g swordfish steak

extra virgin olive oil

24 large bay leaves, soaked in cold water for 1 hour

2 lemons, cut into 24 chunks

freshly squeezed lemon juice, to serve

Moroccan rub

1¹/₂ teaspoons coriander seeds

¹/₂ teaspoon cumin seeds

1 cinnamon stick

¹/₂ teaspoon whole allspice berries

3 cloves

¹/₂ teaspoon ground turmeric

1 teaspoon dried onion flakes

¹/₂ teaspoon sea salt

¹/₄ teaspoon paprika

Couscous

250 g couscous

300 ml boiling water

50 g freshly grated Parmesan cheese

50 g unsalted butter, melted

1 tablespoon chopped fresh thyme

sea salt and freshly ground black pepper

8 wooden skewers, soaked in water for 30 minutes

Serves 4

To make the Moroccan rub, put the whole spices into a dry frying pan and toast over medium heat for about 1–2 minutes or until golden and aromatic. Remove from the heat and leave to cool. Transfer to a spice grinder and crush to a coarse powder. Put the spices into a bowl, add the remaining ingredients and mix well. Set aside to infuse.

Using a sharp knife, cut the swordfish into 32 cubes and put into a shallow ceramic dish. Add a sprinkle of olive oil and the Moroccan rub, toss well until the fish is evenly coated. Leave to marinate in the refrigerator for 1 hour.

About 10 minutes before cooking the fish, put the couscous into a sieve and rinse under cold running water to moisten all the grains, then put into a steamer and steam for 10 minutes or until the grains have softened. Transfer the couscous to a warmed serving dish and immediately stir in the Parmesan cheese, melted butter, thyme and seasonings. Keep the couscous warm.

Preheat the barbecue. Thread the fish, bay leaves and chunks of lemon onto the soaked wooden skewers and barbecue over hot coals for 3–4 minutes, turning halfway through until cooked. Serve the skewers on a bed of couscous, sprinkled with olive oil and lemon juice.

swordfish
with salsa

Swordfish is brought to life with this delicious salsa. Slow-roasting softens the tomatoes and intensifies their flavour. This salsa is great served with many different fish and meat dishes, as well as on a bowl of fresh pasta such as ravioli.

500 g cherry tomatoes

2 red onions, finely chopped

1/2 teaspoon crushed dried chillies

a large bunch of fresh flat leaf parsley, chopped

6 tablespoons olive oil

freshly squeezed juice of 2 limes

8 swordfish steaks, 100 g each

sea salt and freshly ground pepper

Serves 8

Preheat the oven to 150°C (300°F) Gas 2.

To make the salsa, put the tomatoes into a roasting tin and cook in the preheated oven for 1 hour. Remove and leave to cool.

Transfer to a bowl, add the onions, dried chillies, parsley, oil, lime juice, salt and pepper. Mix well.

Preheat the barbecue.

Sprinkle the swordfish steaks with salt and pepper. Cook over medium heat on the preheated barbecue for 4–6 minutes on each side, depending on thickness, until just cooked through. Serve with the salsa.

sesame-crusted marlin
with ginger dressing

Marlin is fantastic for the barbecue, as it is firm and doesn't break up when turned. It's a dense fish with an intense flavour, so serve it in small portions. Swordfish also works well.

20 marlin or swordfish steaks, 100 g each

5 egg whites

750 g toasted sesame seeds

1 tablespoon crushed dried chillies

Ginger dressing

400 g fresh ginger, peeled and finely chopped

600 ml light soy sauce

2 bunches of spring onions, chopped

4 tablespoons toasted sesame oil

Serves 20

Preheat the barbecue.

To make the dressing, put the ginger, soy sauce, spring onions and sesame oil into a bowl and mix.

Dry the marlin steaks with kitchen paper. Put the egg whites into a bowl and whisk until frothy. Put the sesame seeds and dried chillies onto a large plate and mix. Dip each marlin steak first into the egg whites, then into the sesame seeds and dried chillies, until evenly coated on both sides.

Cook on the preheated barbecue for 5 minutes on each side. Spoon the dressing over the marlin and serve.

Even if the snapper has already been scaled by the fishmonger, go over it again to remove any stray scales – they are huge! A fish grilling basket could also be used to cook this fish. Serve with chilled, crisp white or rosé wine and crusty bread.

red snapper with parsley salad

To make the herb, lemon and garlic marinade, strip the rosemary and thyme leaves from the stalk and put into a mortar. Add the bay leaves, garlic and lemon zest and pound with a pestle to release the aromas. Put the mixture into a bowl and add the peppercorns and olive oil.

Using a sharp knife, cut several slashes into each side of the fish. Put into a shallow ceramic dish and add the marinade. Marinate in the refrigerator for 4 hours, but return to room temperature 1 hour before cooking.

Preheat the barbecue.

Just before cooking the fish, make the salad. Put the raisins into a bowl, add the verjuice and leave to soak for 15 minutes. Drain and set the liquid aside. Put the parsley, pine nuts, soaked raisins and feta into a bowl. Put the olive oil, vinegar and reserved raisin liquid into a separate bowl and mix well. Pour over the salad and toss until the leaves are well coated. Season with sea salt and black pepper.

Barbecue the fish over hot coals for 4–5 minutes on each side, leave to rest briefly and serve at once with the parsley salad.

* Verjuice, which is used in the salad dressing, is produced from the juice of unripe grapes. It is available from Italian delicatessens. If you can't find it, use white grape juice instead.

4 red snapper, cleaned and well scaled, about 350 g each

Herb, lemon and garlic marinade

2 sprigs of fresh rosemary

2 sprigs of fresh thyme

4 bay leaves

2 large garlic cloves, coarsely chopped

grated zest of 1 unwaxed lemon

1 teaspoon black peppercorns, coarsely crushed

200 ml extra virgin olive oil

Parsley salad

50 g raisins

2 tablespoons verjuice* or white grape juice

leaves from a large bunch of fresh parsley

25 g pine nuts

50 g feta cheese, crumbled

3 tablespoons extra virgin olive oil

2 teaspoons balsamic vinegar

sea salt and freshly ground black pepper

Serves 4

Smoking food on the barbecue is done using the indirect barbecuing method, so the food cooks more slowly and the flavour of the smoke can penetrate. For smoking, you will need a barbecue with a lid.

hot-smoked creole salmon

4 salmon fillets, skinned, about 200 g each

Creole rub

1/2 small onion, finely chopped

1 garlic clove, finely chopped

1 tablespoon chopped fresh thyme

1 tablespoon paprika

1 teaspoon ground cumin

1 teaspoon sea salt

1/4 teaspoon cayenne pepper

1 tablespoon brown sugar

freshly ground black pepper

Mango and sesame salsa

1 large ripe mango, peeled, stoned and chopped

4 spring onions, chopped

1 fresh red chilli, deseeded and chopped

1 garlic clove, crushed

1 tablespoon light soy sauce

1 tablespoon freshly squeezed lime juice

1 teaspoon sesame oil

1/2 tablespoon sugar

1 tablespoon chopped fresh coriander

sea salt and freshly ground black pepper

a large handful of wood chips, such as hickory, soaked in water for 1 hour, then drained

Serves 4

To make the Creole rub, put all the ingredients into a small bowl, stir well and set aside to infuse until ready to use.

Wash the salmon under cold running water and pat dry with kitchen paper. Using a small pair of tweezers, pull out any bones, then put the fish into a dish and work the Creole rub all over it. Leave to marinate in the refrigerator for at least 1 hour.

To make the salsa, put the chopped mango in a bowl, then add the spring onions, chilli, garlic, soy sauce, lime juice, sesame oil, sugar, coriander, salt and pepper. Mix well and set aside for 30 minutes to let the flavours infuse.

Preheat the charcoal barbecue for indirect barbecuing, according to the manufacturer's instructions. Put a drip tray in the middle and, when the coals are hot, tip half the soaked wood chips onto each pile. Cover with the lid, leaving any air vents open during barbecuing.

As soon as the wood chips start to smoke, put the salmon fillets into the centre of the barbecue, cover and cook for about 15–20 minutes or until the salmon is cooked through.

To test the fish, press the salmon with your finger – the flesh should feel firm and start to open into flakes. Serve hot or cold with the mango and sesame salsa.

A great way to prepare whole salmon is to remove the central bone from the fish, then tie the two fillets back together. If your filleting skills are limited, you could always ask your fishmonger to fillet the whole fish for you.

whole salmon
stuffed with herbs

2 kg whole salmon, filleted

125 g salted butter, softened

25 g chopped, fresh soft-leaf mixed herbs, such as basil, chives, mint, parsley and tarragon

grated zest of 1 unwaxed lemon

1 garlic clove, crushed

sea salt and freshly ground black pepper

olive oil, for brushing

Serves 8

Put the salmon fillets flat onto a board, flesh side up. Carefully pull out any remaining bones with tweezers.

Put the butter, herbs, lemon zest, garlic and plenty of pepper into a small bowl and beat well. Spread the mixture over one of the salmon fillets and put the second on the top, arranging them top to tail.

Using kitchen string, tie the fish together at 2.5 cm intervals. Brush with a little olive oil, sprinkle with salt and freshly ground black pepper and cook on the flat plate of a barbecue for 10 minutes on each side. Leave to rest for a further 10 minutes. Remove the string and serve the fish cut into portions.

peppered tuna steak
with salsa rossa

Salsa rossa is one of those divine Italian sauces that transforms simple meat and fish dishes into food nirvana. The slight sweetness from the peppers is a good foil for the spicy pepper crust.

6 tablespoons mixed peppercorns, coarsely crushed

6 tuna steaks, 200 g each

1 tablespoon extra virgin olive oil

salad leaves, to serve

Salsa rossa

1 large red pepper

1 tablespoon extra virgin olive oil

2 garlic cloves, crushed

2 large ripe tomatoes, peeled and roughly chopped

a small pinch of dried chilli flakes

1 tablespoon dried oregano

1 tablespoon red wine vinegar

sea salt and freshly ground black pepper

Serves 6

To make the salsa rossa, grill the pepper until charred all over, then put into a plastic bag and leave to cool. Remove and discard the skin and seeds, reserving any juices, then chop the flesh.

Put the oil into a frying pan, heat gently, then add the garlic and fry for 3 minutes. Add the tomatoes, chilli flakes and oregano and simmer gently for 15 minutes. Stir in the peppers and the vinegar and simmer for a further 5 minutes to evaporate any excess liquid.

Transfer to a blender and purée until fairly smooth. Add salt and pepper to taste and leave to cool. It may be stored in a screw-top jar in the refrigerator for up to 3 days.

Put the crushed peppercorns onto a large plate. Brush the tuna steaks with olive oil, then press the crushed peppercorns into the surface. Preheat a ridged stove-top grill pan or barbecue until hot, add the tuna and cook for 1 minute on each side. Wrap loosely in foil and leave to rest for 5 minutes before serving with the salsa rossa and a mixed leaves salad.

Dukkah is a Middle Eastern dish comprising mixed nuts and spices, which are ground to a coarse powder and served as a dip for warm bread. For this recipe, it is used as a coating for grilled tuna. Preserved lemons are available from good delicatessens and Middle Eastern food stores.

dukkah-crusted tuna
with preserved lemon salsa

4 tuna steaks, about 200 g each

3 tablespoons sesame seeds

2 tablespoons coriander seeds

1/2 tablespoon cumin seeds

25 g blanched almonds, chopped

1/2 teaspoon salt

freshly ground black pepper

olive oil, for brushing

Preserved lemon salsa

25 g preserved lemons

25 g semi-dried tomatoes

2 spring onions, very finely chopped

1 tablespoon coarsely chopped fresh parsley

3 tablespoons extra virgin olive oil

1/4 teaspoon caster sugar

Serves 4

To make the salsa, chop the preserved lemon and tomatoes finely and put into a bowl. Stir in the spring onions, parsley, olive oil and sugar and set aside until ready to serve.

Preheat the barbecue.

Wash the tuna steaks under cold running water and pat dry with kitchen paper.

Put the sesame seeds into a dry frying pan and toast over medium heat until golden and aromatic. Remove and leave to cool. Repeat with the coriander seeds, cumin seeds and almonds. Transfer to a spice grinder and grind roughly. Alternatively, use a pestle and mortar. Add the salt and a little pepper.

Brush the tuna steaks with olive oil and coat with the dukkah mixture. Cook over hot coals for 1 minute on each side, top with the salsa and serve.

Cooking with the lid on your barbecue creates the same effect as cooking in a conventional oven. If you don't have a barbecue with a lid, you can cut the chicken in half and cook on the grill rack for about 15 minutes on each side.

whole chicken
roasted on the barbecue

1.5 kg chicken

1 lemon, halved

4 garlic cloves, peeled

a small bunch of fresh thyme

extra virgin olive oil

sea salt and freshly ground black pepper

Serves 4–6

Wash the chicken thoroughly under cold running water and pat dry with kitchen paper.

Rub the chicken all over with the halved lemon, then put the lemon halves inside the body cavity with the garlic cloves and thyme. Rub a little olive oil into the skin and season liberally with salt and pepper.

Preheat the barbecue for indirect barbecuing, following the manufacturer's instructions, and put a drip tray in the middle. Brush the grill rack with oil and put the chicken above the drip tray. Cover with the lid, then cook over medium-hot coals for 1 hour or until the skin is golden, the flesh is cooked through and the juices run clear when the thickest part of the meat is pierced with a skewer. If any bloody juices appear, then cook a little longer.

Leave the chicken to rest for 10 minutes before serving.

pepper 'n' spice chicken

Based on the classic Asian salt 'n' pepper squid, this delicious dish is a great way to use up leftover chicken. Serve with a squeeze of lime and the sweet chilli sauce.

1 small chicken

2 tablespoons toasted sesame oil

1–2 limes, cut into wedges

Fragrant Asian rub

4 whole star anise

2 teaspoons Szechuan peppercorns

1 teaspoon fennel seeds

2 small pieces of cassia bark or 1 cinnamon stick, broken

6 cloves

2 garlic cloves, finely chopped

grated zest of 2 unwaxed limes

1 teaspoon sea salt

Sweet chilli sauce

6 large red chillies, deseeded and chopped

4 garlic cloves, chopped

1 teaspoon peeled and grated fresh ginger

1 teaspoon sea salt

100 ml rice wine vinegar

100 g sugar

Serves 4

To make the fragrant Asian rub, put the whole spices into a dry frying pan and toast over medium heat for 1–2 minutes or until golden and aromatic. Remove from the heat and leave to cool. Transfer to a spice grinder and crush to a coarse powder. Put the spices into a bowl, add the garlic, lime zest and salt and mix well. Set aside to infuse until ready to use.

To make the sweet chilli sauce, put the chillies, garlic, ginger and salt into a food processor and blend to a coarse paste. Transfer to a saucepan, add the vinegar and sugar, bring to the boil and simmer gently, part-covered, for 5 minutes until the mixture becomes a thin syrup. Remove from the heat and leave to cool.

Cut the chicken into 12 portions and put into a dish. Add the rub and sesame oil and work well into the chicken pieces. Leave to marinate in the refrigerator for 2 hours, but return to room temperature for 1 hour before cooking.

Preheat the barbecue, then cook the chicken over medium hot coals for 15–20 minutes, turning after 10 minutes, until the chicken is cooked through and the juices run clear when the thickest part of the meat is pierced with a skewer. Squeeze over some lime juice, leave to cool slightly and serve with the sweet chilli sauce.

2 duck breast fillets, about 200 g each

1 tablespoon salt

2 tablespoons honey

2 tablespoons dark soy sauce

1/2 teaspoon ground star anise

12 Vietnamese ricepaper wrappers

1/2 cucumber, cut into strips

a few fresh herb leaves,
such as coriander, mint and Thai basil

Asian barbecue sauce

100 ml tomato passata

50 ml hoisin sauce

1 teaspoon hot chilli sauce

2 garlic cloves, crushed

2 tablespoons sweet soy sauce

1 tablespoon rice wine vinegar

1 teaspoon ground coriander

1/2 teaspoon ground cinnamon

1/4 teaspoon Chinese five-spice pepper

Serves 4

This dish is similar to the famous Peking duck but takes much less time to prepare. Cooking duck on the barbecue is best done by the indirect method, where the coals are pushed to the sides and a drip tray placed underneath to catch the fat.

barbecue duck ricepaper rolls

To make the Asian barbecue sauce, put all the ingredients into a small saucepan, add 100 ml water, bring to the boil and simmer gently for 10 minutes. Remove from the heat and leave to cool. Pour into an airtight container and store in the refrigerator for up to 2 weeks.

Using a sharp knife, cut several slashes into the duck skin. Rub the skin with the salt and put in a shallow dish. Put the honey, soy sauce and ground star anise into a bowl and mix well. Pour over the duck. Leave to marinate in a cool place for at least 1 hour.

Set up the barbecue for indirect grilling, following the manufacturer's instructions, and put a drip tray in the middle. Cook the duck breast for 15 minutes or until well browned and firm to the touch, leave to rest for 5 minutes, then cut into thin strips and set aside until required.

Put the ricepaper wrappers into a large bowl of cold water, leave to soak until softened, then pat dry and spread flat on the work surface. Put a few slices of duck, some strips of cucumber and herbs into the middle of each wrapper and add a little of the barbecue sauce.

Fold the ends of the wrapper over the duck and roll up the sides to enclose the filling. Transfer to a large platter and serve with the barbecue sauce.

A good burger should be thick, moist, tender and juicy. These lamb burgers are all that and more. Serve in crusty rolls with a few slices of tomato, plenty of fresh salad leaves and a generous spoonful of the cool minty yoghurt dressing. The perfect burger for a barbecue party.

lamb burgers
with mint yoghurt

650 g boneless lamb shoulder, cut into 2 cm cubes

100 g pork belly, chopped

1 onion, very finely chopped

2 garlic cloves, crushed

2 tablespoons ground cumin

2 teaspoons ground cinnamon

1 tablespoon dried oregano

2 teaspoons salt

50 g fresh breadcrumbs

1 tablespoon capers, drained and chopped

freshly ground black pepper

1 large egg, beaten

4 crusty rolls, to serve

salad leaves, to serve

tomato slices, to serve

Mint yoghurt

200 g thick yoghurt

2 tablespoons chopped fresh mint

sea salt and freshly ground black pepper

Serves 4

Put the lamb and pork into a food processor and process briefly until coarsely ground. Transfer to a bowl and, using your hands, work in the chopped onion, garlic, cumin, cinnamon, oregano, salt, breadcrumbs, capers, pepper and beaten egg. Cover and marinate in the refrigerator for at least 2 hours

Preheat the barbecue.

Put the yoghurt into a bowl and stir in the mint, then add a little salt and pepper to taste. Set aside until required.

Using damp hands, shape the meat into 8 burgers. Brush the grill rack with oil. Barbecue the burgers for about 3 minutes on each side.

Split the rolls in half and fill with the cooked burgers, salad leaves, tomato slices and a spoonful of mint yoghurt.

Variation For a traditional hamburger, replace the lamb with beef, omit the spices and, instead of the capers, add 4 chopped anchovy fillets. Serve in burger buns with salad.

Souvlaki is the classic Greek kebab, a delicious combination of cubed lamb marinated in red wine with herbs and lemon juice – a juicy and succulent dish.

souvlaki
with cracked wheat salad

1 kg neck end of lamb

1 tablespoon chopped fresh rosemary

1 tablespoon dried oregano

1 onion, chopped

4 garlic cloves, chopped

300 ml red wine

freshly squeezed juice of 1 lemon

75 ml olive oil

sea salt and freshly ground black pepper

Cracked wheat salad

350 g cracked wheat (bulghur wheat)

25 g fresh flat leaf parsley

15 g fresh mint leaves

2 garlic cloves, crushed

150 ml extra virgin olive oil

freshly squeezed juice of 2 lemons

a pinch of caster sugar

sea salt and and freshly ground black pepper

6 large rosemary stalks or metal skewers

Serves 6

Trim any large pieces of fat from the lamb and then cut the meat into 2.5 cm cubes. Put into a shallow, non-metal dish. Add the rosemary, oregano, onion, garlic, wine, lemon juice, olive oil, salt and pepper. Toss well, cover and leave to marinate in the refrigerator for 4 hours. Return to room temperature for 1 hour before cooking.

To make the salad, soak the cracked wheat in warm water for 30 minutes until the water has been absorbed and the grains have softened. Strain well to extract any excess water and transfer the wheat to a bowl. Add all the remaining ingredients, season to taste and set aside for 30 minutes to develop the flavours.

Preheat the barbecue. Thread the lamb onto the rosemary stalks or skewers. Cook on the preheated barbecue for 10 minutes, turning and basting from time to time. Leave to rest for 5 minutes, then serve with the salad.

butterflied leg of lamb
with cumin, lemon and garlic

A butterflied leg of lamb, where the bone is removed and the meat opened up to create a huge flat piece of meat, is one of the tastiest, simplest and most impressive dishes to barbecue. Order it in advance from a butcher and he'll do all the hard work for you. Serve with Kisir (page 40), a mixed green salad and some flatbreads.

2 large garlic cloves, chopped

1 teaspoon sea salt

1 tablespoon cumin seeds

1 teaspoon coriander seeds

1 teaspoon herbes de Provence

1/2 teaspoon black peppercorns

1/4 teaspoon crushed chillies

freshly squeezed juice of 1 lemon

3 tablespoons olive oil

1 large butterflied leg of lamb (about 2–2.5 kg)

a large roasting tin

Serves 8

Put the garlic, salt, cumin seeds, coriander seeds, herbes de Provence, black peppercorns and chillies in a mortar and pound with a pestle until the garlic breaks down and you have a thick paste. Gradually work in the lemon juice and olive oil. Work over the meat with a small, sharp knife, cutting away any excess fat, then cut the meat into 2 or 3 manageable pieces. Put the meat in a roasting tin, rub in the marinade, cover and leave in a cool place for at least 2 hours.

Preheat the barbecue.

Barbecue the lamb for 15–20 minutes, depending on the thickness of the meat and your preference, turning it halfway through the cooking time. Remove to a warmed carving plate, cover with foil and leave to rest for 15 minutes before slicing thinly.

500 g minced pork

125 g pork belly, minced

25 g breadcrumbs

1 stalk of lemongrass, trimmed and tough outer layer discarded, very finely chopped

6 kaffir lime leaves, very thinly sliced

2 garlic cloves, crushed

2 cm fresh ginger, peeled and grated

1 fresh red chilli, deseeded and chopped

2 tablespoons Thai fish sauce

lettuce leaves, to serve

a handful of fresh herb leaves, such as mint, coriander and Thai basil, to serve

Sweet Chilli Sauce (page 71), to serve

4 wooden skewers, soaked in water for 30 minutes

Serves 4

These delicious pork balls are served wrapped in a lettuce leaf with plenty of fresh herbs and sweet chilli sauce.

vietnamese pork balls

Put the minced pork, pork belly and breadcrumbs into a bowl, then add the lemongrass, lime leaves, garlic, ginger, chilli and fish sauce and mix well. Leave to marinate in the refrigerator for 1 hour.

Preheat the barbecue. Shape the mixture into 20 small balls and carefully thread 5 onto each of the soaked wooden skewers. Brush the barbecue rack with oil. Cook the skewers over hot coals for 5–6 minutes, turning halfway through, until cooked.

Serve the pork balls wrapped in the lettuce leaves with the herbs and sweet chilli sauce.

An essential sauce used for the smoky ribs recipe opposite.

barbecue sauce

200 ml tomato passata

100 ml maple syrup

50 ml dark treacle

50 ml tomato ketchup

50 ml white wine vinegar

3 tablespoons Worcestershire sauce

1 tablespoon Dijon mustard

1 teaspoon garlic powder

1/4 teaspoon hot paprika

sea salt and freshly ground pepper

Put all the ingredients in a small saucepan, bring to the boil and simmer gently for 10–15 minutes until reduced slightly and thickened. Season and leave to cool.

2 racks pork spare ribs, about 650 g each

300 ml white wine vinegar

2 tablespoons soft brown sugar

1 tablespoon salt

1 tablespoon sweet paprika

2 teaspoons crushed black pepper

2 teaspoons onion powder

1 teaspoon garlic powder

1/4 teaspoon cayenne pepper

150 ml Barbecue Sauce (page 76)

coleslaw, to serve

Serves 4

These grilled ribs are spicy, smoky, sticky, tender and lip-smackingly good. They may take a little time to prepare because of soaking and marinating, but they are simple to cook and definitely well worth the effort.

smoky barbecue ribs

Wash the ribs under cold running water and pat dry with kitchen paper. Put the ribs into a large dish, add the vinegar and leave to soak for 4 hours or overnight. Rinse the ribs well and pat dry with kitchen paper.

Put the sugar, salt, paprika, pepper, onion powder, garlic powder and cayenne into a bowl and mix well. Rub the mixture all over the ribs and leave to marinate in the refrigerator for 2 hours.

Preheat the barbecue. Cook the ribs over low heat for 20 minutes on each side. Brush with the barbecue sauce and cook for a further 15 minutes on each side until the ribs are lightly charred, tender and sticky. Remove and leave to cool briefly before serving with coleslaw.

Ripe figs filled with goats' cheese, then wrapped in prosciutto, make a great first course at an alfresco supper. Prepare the salad in advance, but add the dressing at the last minute, otherwise it may become soggy.

fig, goats' cheese and prosciutto skewers
with radicchio salad

Using a sharp knife, cut each fig lengthways into quarters without cutting all the way through. Cut the cheese into 8 equal pieces, put into the middle of each fig and close the figs. Wrap each fig with a slice of the ham and thread carefully onto the soaked wooden skewers.

Preheat the barbecue, then cook the skewers over medium-hot coals for 4–5 minutes, turning halfway through until the ham is charred and the figs are sizzling.

To make the salad, tear the radicchio leaves into pieces and put into a bowl with the walnuts. Put the remaining ingredients into a separate bowl and whisk well. Pour the dressing over the leaves and toss until coated. Serve with the skewers.

* To reduce balsamic vinegar, put 300 ml into a saucepan and boil gently until reduced by about two-thirds and the consistency of thick syrup. Leave to cool, then store in a clean jar or bottle.

8 large ripe figs

80 g goats' cheese

8 slices prosciutto

Radicchio salad

1 head of radicchio, trimmed

a handful of walnut pieces, lightly toasted in a dry frying pan

4 tablespoons walnut oil

2 tablespoons extra virgin olive oil

1 tablespoon vincotto or reduced balsamic vinegar*

sea salt and freshly ground black pepper

4 wooden skewers, soaked in water for 30 minutes

Serves 4

150 g bread

5 tablespoons milk

800 g minced pork

2 eggs

a handful of fresh parsley, finely chopped

4 garlic cloves, crushed

1 teaspoon ground cinnamon

a large pinch of ground cloves

1 teaspoon ground turmeric

a large pinch of chilli powder

seeds of 4 cardamom pods, crushed

1 teaspoon sea salt

freshly ground black pepper

olive oil, for brushing

tomato chutney, to serve (optional)

6 pita breads, to serve

150 g shredded iceberg lettuce, to serve

300 ml natural set yoghurt, to serve

Serves 4–6

No barbecue – especially where children are involved – is complete without burgers, but burgers don't necessarily have to mean junk food. Not only is it healthier to make your own, but fun too, as you can experiment with herbs and spices. This recipe can be varied to use beef, lamb or poultry, but make sure that you use good-quality meat. The addition of bread to the mixture gives a smoother texture and flavour.

aromatic pork burger in pita bread

Soak the bread in the milk for 10–15 minutes until soft, then squeeze the bread with your hands until it is almost dry and put in a bowl. Add the minced pork, eggs, parsley, garlic, spices, salt and plenty of pepper. Mix well, cover and leave to stand for 60 minutes.

Shape the meat mixture into 12 burgers. Cover and refrigerate until required.

Preheat the barbecue.

When ready to cook, brush the burgers lightly with olive oil and cook them on the preheated hot barbecue for 20 minutes, turning them from time to time to avoid burning. Cut into one of the burgers to make sure it is cooked in the middle – if it is still pink, cook for an extra 5–10 minutes. Transfer the burgers to a plate. Spread each one with a spoonful of tomato chutney, if using.

Heat the pita breads on the barbecue until just warm. Cut each one in half, open and fill with lettuce, yoghurt and a burger, then serve.

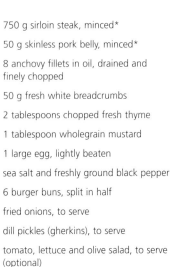

750 g sirloin steak, minced*

50 g skinless pork belly, minced*

8 anchovy fillets in oil, drained and finely chopped

50 g fresh white breadcrumbs

2 tablespoons chopped fresh thyme

1 tablespoon wholegrain mustard

1 large egg, lightly beaten

sea salt and freshly ground black pepper

6 burger buns, split in half

fried onions, to serve

dill pickles (gherkins), to serve

tomato, lettuce and olive salad, to serve (optional)

Serves 6

best-ever beef burger

There are many burger recipes and everyone has their favourite. This one is best served in a bun, with pickles and sauce and a simple salad of tomatoes, lettuce and olives.

Put the minced steak and pork into a bowl and add the anchovies, breadcrumbs, thyme, mustard, beaten egg, salt and pepper, working it with your hands to make a nice, sticky mixture. Shape into 6 burgers and chill for 1 hour.

Preheat the barbecue. Cook the burgers on the preheated barbecue for about 4 minutes on each side. Remove from the heat and leave to rest for 5 minutes. Serve in a bun, with fried onions, dill pickles and the tomato, lettuce and olive salad, if using.

* To make the burger mince, ask your butcher to put the beef and pork through a meat mincer. Alternatively, put it into a food processor and pulse briefly to make a slightly coarse mince.

If you can find porcini mushrooms, all the better, but any field mushrooms will taste great cooked on the barbecue.

whole beef fillet with mushrooms

500 g fillet of beef

1 tablespoon extra virgin olive oil, plus extra for brushing

1 tablespoon crushed black peppercorns

8 large porcini or portobello mushrooms

sea salt and freshly ground black pepper

Beetroot and Baby Onion Brochettes (page 56), to serve (optional)

Dressing

100 ml extra virgin olive oil

1 garlic clove, chopped

1 tablespoon chopped fresh parsley

a squeeze of fresh lemon juice

Serves 4

Brush the beef with olive oil, press the peppercorns into the meat, then sprinkle with salt.

Preheat the barbecue to high. Cook the beef for 15 minutes for rare, 20 minutes for medium and 25 minutes for well done, turning every 5 minutes or so until evenly browned on all sides. Transfer the beef to a roasting tin, cover with foil and leave to rest for 10 minutes.

Brush the mushrooms with olive oil, season with salt and pepper, then put stem side down on the grill rack and barbecue for 5 minutes on each side. Transfer the mushrooms to the roasting tin and leave to rest for a further 1–2 minutes.

Meanwhile, put all the dressing ingredients into a bowl and mix well. Serve the beef in thick slices with the mushrooms, a sprinkle of the dressing and the beetroot and baby onion brochettes, if using.

main courses

quiche lorraine

This is the classic tart from Alsace and Lorraine, and the forerunner of many copies. Made well and with the best ingredients, this simplest of dishes is food fit for the gods, especially when a little grated Gruyère is added to the filling. The quantities given for the pastry are generous – any left over may be frozen or used to make tartlets. Making the pastry by hand is the best method because more air will be incorporated, but if you have hot hands, the food processor is a blessing!

200 g bacon lardons or cubed pancetta

5 eggs

200 ml double cream or crème fraîche

freshly grated nutmeg, to taste

50 g Gruyère cheese, grated

sea salt and freshly ground black pepper

Shortcrust pastry

250 g plain flour

a pinch of salt

50 g lard (or white cooking fat), chilled and diced

75 g unsalted butter, chilled and diced

2–3 tablespoons chilled water

a tart tin, 23 cm diameter

baking beans

Serves 4–6

Preheat the oven to 200°C (400°F) Gas 6.

To make the pastry, sift the flour and salt together into a bowl. (Alternatively, sift into a food processor.)

Rub in the lard and butter until the mixture resembles breadcrumbs. (Or add to the food processor and blend for 30 seconds for the same result.)

Add the water, mixing lightly with a knife to bring the pastry together. (Or add to the food processor, and pulse for 10 seconds until the pastry forms large lumps. Add another tablespoon of water and repeat if necessary.)

Knead lightly on a floured work surface, then shape into a flattened ball, wrap in clingfilm and chill for at least 30 minutes before rolling out.

Bring the pastry to room temperature. Roll out the pastry thinly on a lightly floured work surface and use to line the tart tin. Prick the base, chill or freeze for 15 minutes.

Spread foil over the tin, letting it hang over the sides, then fill the tin with baking beans. Set on a baking tray and bake blind in the centre of the oven for about 10–12 minutes.

Remove the foil and baking beans and return the pastry case to the oven for a further 5–7 minutes to dry out completely.

To prevent the pastry from becoming soggy when the filling is added, brush the baked-blind case with beaten egg. Bake again for 5–10 minutes until set and shiny. This will also fill and seal any holes made when pricking the pastry before the blind baking.

If necessary, repeat the sealing process until an impervious layer has been built. Put the pastry to one side.

Heat a non-stick frying pan and fry the bacon or pancetta until brown and crisp, then drain on kitchen paper. Scatter over the pastry case.

Put the eggs and cream into a bowl, beat well, and season with salt, pepper and nutmeg to taste. Carefully pour the mixture over the bacon and sprinkle with the Gruyère.

Bake for about 25 minutes until just set, golden brown and puffy. Serve warm or at room temperature.

This amazingly savoury Ligurian focaccia is topped with a concentrated sauce of tomatoes, salted anchovies or salted sardines (hence the name), and whole melting cloves of garlic. It is perfect for outdoor eating, served in thin slices with a cold glass of wine or beer.

sardenaira

25 g fresh yeast

1/2 teaspoon sugar

150 ml warm milk

500 g Italian '00' flour

7 tablespoons extra virgin olive oil

100 ml hand-hot water

2 onions, thinly sliced

1 kg fresh, very ripe tomatoes, peeled and chopped, or 1 kg (drained weight) tinned whole tomatoes

100 g anchovies or sardines in salt

12 or more whole garlic cloves, unpeeled

100 g or more small stoned black Ligurian olives

1 tablespoon dried oregano

sea salt and freshly ground black pepper

a 28 x 43 x 2.5 cm baking tin, oiled

Serves 10

In a large bowl, cream the fresh yeast with the sugar and whisk in the warm milk. Leave for 10 minutes until frothy.

Sift the flour with 1 teaspoon salt into a large bowl and make a well in the centre. Pour in the yeast mixture, 4 tablespoons of the olive oil and the water. Mix together with a round-bladed knife, then use your hands until the dough comes together. Tip out onto a lightly floured surface, then knead briskly for 10–15 minutes until smooth, shiny and elastic. Try not to add any extra flour at this stage – a wetter dough is better. If you feel the dough is sticky, flour your hands and not the dough. The dough should be quite soft. If it is really too soft to handle, knead in a little more flour.

To test if the dough is ready, roll it into a fat sausage, take each end in either hand, lift the dough up and pull and stretch the dough outwards, gently wiggling it up and down – it should stretch out quite easily. If it doesn't, it needs more kneading. Shape into a neat ball. Put it in an oiled bowl, cover with clingfilm or a damp tea towel and leave to rise in a warm, draught-free place until doubled in size – about 1½ hours.

Preheat the oven to 180°C (350°F) Gas 4.

Heat the remaining olive oil in a large saucepan, add the onions and cook for about 10 minutes until beginning to soften and colour slightly. Add the tomatoes and cook gently until collapsed and very thick. Meanwhile, split the anchovies, remove the backbone, rinse and roughly chop. Stir into the sauce and season to taste.

Knock back the dough, knead lightly, then stretch and pat it out into the prepared tin, pushing the dough well up the edges. Spread the sauce on top of the dough, cover with the whole garlic cloves and the olives, then sprinkle with the oregano. Drizzle with a little olive oil and bake for about 1 hour until the focaccia is golden. Serve sliced – hot, warm or cold.

roquefort and walnut tart

Blue cheese imparts a wonderful richness of flavour to this light creamy tart made with walnut pastry. Served with a salad made from rocket, pears and walnuts, it is a delicious main course for an alfresco lunch.

To make the pastry, put the walnuts into a dry frying pan and cook for 1–2 minutes until they start to smell toasted. Transfer to a bowl and leave to cool.

Transfer to a food processor or blender and grind to a meal. Sift the flour and salt into a bowl and rub in the butter until the mixture resembles fine breadcrumbs. Stir in the ground walnuts and then enough cold water to form a soft dough. Transfer the dough to a lightly floured surface, knead gently, then shape into a flat disc. Wrap in clingfilm and chill for about 30 minutes.

Preheat the oven to 200°C (400°F) Gas 6.

Transfer the dough to a lightly floured surface, roll out to a disc about 25 cm in diameter and use to line the flan tin. Prick the base with a fork and chill for a further 30 minutes. Remove from the refrigerator and line the pastry case with parchment paper and baking beans. Bake in the preheated oven for 10 minutes. Remove the paper and beans and bake for a further 5–6 minutes until the pastry is crisp and lightly golden. Remove from the oven and leave to cool for about 10 minutes.

To make the filling, dice the Roquefort and put into a food processor. Add the ricotta, cream, eggs, walnut oil, salt and pepper and blend briefly until mixed but not smooth. Pour into the pastry case and cook for about 20 minutes until risen and golden. Leave to cool slightly in the tin, then serve warm.

To make the salad, put the walnuts into a dry frying pan and toast until golden. Remove, cool and chop coarsely. Peel, core and slice the pears and put into a bowl. Add the rocket, parsley and walnuts.

Put the walnut oil into a measuring cup, add the olive oil, sherry vinegar, honey, salt and pepper and whisk well. Pour over the salad, toss gently, then serve with the tart.

Pastry

15 g shelled walnuts

100 g plain flour

1 teaspoon salt

50 g unsalted butter, diced

Roquefort filling

100 g Roquefort cheese

200 g ricotta cheese

150 ml double cream

3 eggs, lightly beaten

2 tablespoons walnut oil

salt and pepper

Rocket salad

50 g shelled walnuts

2 ripe pears

200 g rocket

a handful of fresh flat leaf parsley

4 tablespoons walnut oil

2 tablespoons olive oil

2 teaspoons sherry vinegar

1 teaspoon clear honey

salt and pepper

23 cm flan tin, greased

baking beans

Serves 6

250 g plain flour

1/2 sachet easy-blend dried yeast (3.5 g)

1/2 teaspoon salt

150 ml lukewarm water

Topping

4 tablespoons extra virgin olive oil

350 g red onions, cut into wedges

about 500 g tinned piquillo peppers, drained

leaves from a small handful of fresh thyme
or rosemary sprigs

2 tablespoons anchovy paste or purée, or tinned
anchovies, chopped and mashed

16 marinated anchovy fillets

a baking tray, oiled

Serves 4–6

To make the dough, put the flour, yeast and
salt in a bowl and mix. Add the water and
mix to a satiny dough, then knead, still in the
bowl, for 5 minutes or until silky. Cover the
bowl with a cloth and leave for about 1 hour
or until the dough has doubled in size.

Preheat the oven to 220°C (425°F) Gas 7.

Meanwhile, to make the topping, heat
3 tablespoons of the oil in a frying pan, add
the onions and cook, stirring over medium
heat until softened and transparent. Slice
half the piquillos and add to the pan. Stir
in most of the herbs.

Transfer the dough to the prepared baking
tray. Punch down, flatten and roll out the
dough to a circle 30 cm in diameter. Snip,
twist or roll the edges. Spread the anchovy
paste all over the top. Add the remaining
piquillos, left whole, and the cooked
onion mixture. Arrange the anchovies and
remaining herbs in a decorative pattern
on top and sprinkle with the remaining oil.

Bake in the preheated oven for
25–30 minutes until the base is crisp
and risen, the edges golden and the filling
hot and wilted. Serve in wedges, hot
or cool.

A novel way of serving this traditional Spanish dish is to cut it into uneven chunks
and pile it hot and high on plates. Served with olives and glasses of chilled white
wine, it makes a tasty tapas dish for a picnic. If you haven't any piquillo peppers,
use tinned pimiento or grilled or roasted fresh red peppers.

spanish tart
with peppers

leek, feta and black olive tart
with endive and watercress salad and spiced walnuts

This tart can be made with a multitude of complementary toppings: onion, thyme and blue cheese; wild mushroom and goats' cheese; or spinach, ricotta and pine nuts. It is quite substantial, so take advantage of the vast array of leaves now available and serve with a tasty but light salad. Slightly bitter salad leaves cut through the richness of the tart very well.

Leek tart

375 g ready-made puff pastry, defrosted if frozen

1 tablespoon olive oil

400 g leeks, thinly sliced

a large handful of fresh dill, coarsely chopped

200 g feta cheese, cut into small cubes

100 g stoned black olives

sea salt

a baking tin, about 30 x 20 cm

Serves 4–6

Preheat the oven to 200°C (400°F) Gas 6.

Roll out the pastry to fit the tin almost exactly. Trim and discard a tiny strip around the edge of the pastry so that it will rise evenly.

Heat a wok or frying pan, add the oil and leeks and stir-fry. Add just a little salt, then stir in the dill. Transfer to a colander to drain. Cool.

Arrange the leeks over the base of the pastry. Top with the feta and olives. Bake in the preheated oven for 35 minutes, or until the pastry has risen and is golden brown.

Serve with the endive and watercress salad (right).

Endive and watercress salad

100 g shelled walnuts

1 tablespoon soy sauce

1 teaspoon chilli oil

2 heads of chicory, halved lengthways

freshly squeezed juice of 1/2 lime

175 g watercress

1 small head of radicchio, cored and shredded

30 g dried mango, soaked overnight, then sliced into long strips

Dressing

150 ml soured cream

1 tablespoon freshly squeezed lemon juice

2 teaspoons truffle oil (optional)

1 garlic clove, crushed

sea salt and freshly ground black pepper

Serves 4–6

Preheat the oven to 200°C (400°F) Gas 6.

Put the walnuts on a baking tray and roast in the centre of the preheated oven for 15 minutes or until golden and aromatic. Sprinkle with soy sauce and chilli oil, toss well, then return to the oven for a further 10 minutes. Leave to cool.

Cut the chicory into long strips and put in a large salad bowl. Add the lime juice and toss to prevent discoloration. Add the walnuts, watercress, radicchio and mango strips.

Mix the dressing ingredients in a small bowl and serve separately so that the colours of the salad won't be masked by the soured cream.

Tomatoes bursting with flavour, garlic softly singing and layers of crisp pastry melting in every mouthful – what could be simpler or more delicious than this tart?

tomato upside-down tart
with basil

Preheat the oven to 160°C (325°F) Gas 3.

Cut the tomatoes in half around the middle. Arrange cut side up in the tart tin, so that they fit tightly together. Mix the garlic and oregano with the olive oil, salt and pepper. Spoon or brush the mixture over the cut tomatoes.

Bake in the preheated oven for about 2 hours, checking from time to time – the tomatoes should be slightly shrunk and still a brilliant red colour. If too dark, they will be bitter. Leave to cool in the tin (if the tin is very burned, wash it out, brush it with oil and return the tomatoes). Increase the oven temperature to 200°C (400°F) Gas 6.

Roll out the pastry to a circle slightly bigger than the tin. Using the rolling pin to help you, lift up the pastry and unroll it over the tin, letting the edges drape over the sides. Lightly press the pastry down over the tomatoes, but do not trim the edges yet. Bake for 20 minutes until golden.

Leave to settle for 5 minutes, then trim off the overhanging edges and invert onto a plate. Sprinkle with olive oil and basil leaves and serve.

8–10 large ripe plum tomatoes (size depending on what will fit the tin)

2 garlic cloves, finely chopped

1 tablespoon dried oregano

4 tablespoons extra virgin olive oil, plus extra to serve

250 g ready-made puff pastry, defrosted if frozen

sea salt and freshly ground black pepper

a good handful of fresh basil leaves, to serve

a shallow tart tin, 22 cm diameter

Serves 4

Caramelized onions smell just divine, especially when cooked in butter. These simple onion tarts, topped with creamy goats' cheese, are best served warm, although they are also good cold.

onion, thyme and goats' cheese tarts

40 g salted butter

500 g onions, thinly sliced

2 garlic cloves, crushed

1 tablespoon chopped fresh thyme leaves

350 g ready-made puff pastry, defrosted if frozen

flour, for rolling out

200 g log goats' cheese

sea salt and freshly ground black pepper

Makes 8

Preheat the oven to 220°C (425°F) Gas 7.

Put the butter into a frying pan, melt over low heat, then add the onion, garlic and thyme and fry gently for 20–25 minutes, until softened and golden. Leave to cool.

Put the pastry onto a lightly floured surface and roll out to form a rectangle, 20 x 40 cm, trimming the edges. Cut the rectangle in half lengthways and into 4 crossways, making 8 pieces, about 10 cm square.

Divide the onion mixture between the squares, spreading it over the top, leaving a thin border around the edges. Cut the cheese into 8 slices and arrange in the centre of each square.

Transfer the pastries to a large baking tray and bake in the preheated oven for about 12–15 minutes until the pastry has risen and the cheese is golden. Leave to cool a little, then serve warm.

Although this pie looks and tastes quite exotic, it is very simple and quick to make. The recipe calls for a jar of ready-made pesto, but if you make your own pesto, it will be even more delicious (see page 95). It's a must for a fancy picnic. You can use white fish instead of salmon.

layered salmon, prawn and potato filo pie

Cook the potatoes in salted boiling water for 20–30 minutes or until tender. Drain and leave to cool.

Heat enough olive oil to cover the base of a large saucepan over medium heat. Add the tomatoes, garlic and chilli, reduce the heat to low, then cover and simmer for 30 minutes, stirring from time to time to ensure the sauce does not stick. Mash the tomatoes to a pulp using a potato masher. Season the salmon with salt and pepper, then add to the saucepan for 1–2 minutes to lightly cook. Transfer the sauce to a bowl and leave to cool. Slice the potatoes lengthways, then put in a bowl with the pesto and toss to coat evenly.

Preheat the oven to 200°C (400°F) Gas 6.

Brush the base and sides of the cake tin with a little of the melted butter. Brush a sheet of filo pastry with melted butter and lay it across the cake tin to line the base and sides of the tin, leaving any excess hanging over the sides. Brush another sheet of filo pastry with butter and lay it at right angles to the first sheet, smoothing it down to line the base and sides of the tin. There should now be an equal overhang of filo all the way round the tin. Repeat with the remaining sheets of pastry, reserving a little of the butter.

Cover the base of the pie with half the potato mixture, followed by half the sauce and half the prawns. Make a second layer of each and then carefully fold the overhang of pastry over the filling. Brush the top of the pie with the remaining melted butter.

Set the tin on a baking tray and cook in the preheated oven for 25 minutes until golden brown.

If you are going on a picnic immediately, leave to cool slightly in the tin, then wrap in a clean tea towel. Otherwise, leave to cool completely, wrap in aluminium foil and refrigerate until required. Serve with a green salad.

500 g new potatoes

2 x 400-g tins chopped tomatoes, drained

2 garlic cloves, crushed

1 small piece of dried chilli, to taste

500 g salmon fillet, skin removed, cut lengthways into medium-sized chunks

100–150 g Pesto (page 95)

100 g salted butter, melted

6 large sheets of filo pastry

200 g cooked peeled prawns

sea salt and freshly ground black pepper

olive oil, for frying

green salad, to serve

a springform cake tin, 22 cm in diameter

Serves 6–8

6 red peppers, halved and deseeded

1 tablespoon extra virgin olive oil

250 g soft goats' cheese

125 g mascarpone

2 tablespoons freshly squeezed lemon juice

3 tablespoons capers

2 tablespoons chopped fresh dill, plus extra to garnish

¼ teaspoon freshly ground black pepper

slices of crusty bread, and green salad, to serve

a 25-cm loaf tin

Serves 6–8

This colourful terrine is perfect fare for a summer picnic. Make sure it is kept cold, as it will be difficult to slice at room temperature.

piquant goats' cheese and grilled red pepper terrine

Put the pepper halves, cut side down, on a baking tray and place directly under a very hot grill until charred. Put the peppers in a bowl, cover with a lid or clingfilm and leave to sweat for 10 minutes.

Line the loaf tin with clingfilm, leaving a generous overhang. Peel off and discard the charred skin from the peppers. Cut the peppers in half lengthways and toss with the olive oil. Line the loaf tin with the pepper strips – depending on the height of your tin, they may not come all the way up the sides, which is fine.

In a bowl, mash the goats' cheese, mascarpone and lemon juice to a smooth consistency. Add the capers, dill and pepper and fold through. Pile the cheese mixture into the lined tin. Fold over the peppers and then the clingfilm and press down firmly. Refrigerate for at least 4 hours or overnight if you can.

To serve, unfold the clingfilm and turn the terrine onto a serving plate. Peel off the clingfilm. Sprinkle the top with a little chopped dill. Slice and serve with crusty bread and a green salad.

stuffed picnic loaf

Packed with barbecued vegetables, pesto and goats' cheese, this loaf is great for a picnic. Make it a day ahead so it can be 'pressed' overnight in the refrigerator, allowing the flavours to develop and mingle.

1 round loaf of bread, about 23 cm in diameter, 10 cm high

2 tablespoons extra virgin olive oil

½ quantity Pesto (page 95)

2 large red onions

2 large red peppers

2 large courgettes

250 g soft goats' cheese, cubed

12 large fresh basil leaves

sea salt and freshly ground black pepper

Serves 6

Cut the top off the loaf and carefully scoop out most of the bread, leaving just the outer shell (reserve the bread and make into crumbs for another dish). Put 1 tablespoon of the oil into a bowl, stir in the pesto and spread half the mixture around the inside of the shell and lid. Set aside.

Cut the onions into wedges, brush with a little of the remaining tablespoon of oil and cook on a preheated barbecue or on a ridged stove-top grill pan for 10 minutes on each side until very tender. Leave to cool.

Chargrill the peppers on a preheated barbecue or ridged stove-top grill pan or under a grill for about 15 minutes until blackened all over. Transfer to a plastic bag and leave to cool. Peel away the skin, discard the seeds and cut the flesh into quarters, reserving any juices.

Cut the courgettes lengthways into 2 mm thick slices, brush with oil and barbecue or grill as above for 2–3 minutes each side until lightly charred and softened. Leave to cool.

Arrange the filling in layers inside the loaf, with the goats' cheese and remaining pesto in the middle and the basil on top. Sprinkle with any remaining oil and the pepper juices and replace the lid.

Wrap the whole loaf in clingfilm and put onto a plate. Top with a board and a heavy food tin to weigh it down. Chill in the refrigerator overnight.

To serve, cut into wedges.

roasted vegetable and ricotta loaf

This loaf looks splendid displayed whole before being sliced. The cross-section looks good, too – a vision of colourful vegetables interwoven with creamy ricotta. It keeps well in the refrigerator for a couple of days.

Preheat the oven to 200°C (400°F) Gas 6.

Put the slices of aubergine on a baking tray, brush with olive oil and sprinkle with salt and pepper. Put the tray in the hottest part of the oven and roast for 20–25 minutes until the aubergine is tender. Put the red and yellow peppers and courgettes on the other baking tray, sprinkle with salt, and roast for about 20 minutes or until the peppers begin to blister and the courgettes are tender.

While all the vegetables are roasting, mix the ricotta with the lemon juice, garlic, parsley, chilli, salt and pepper.

When the aubergines are cooked, add the vinegar. Put a damp cloth or clingfilm over the peppers and set aside for 5–10 minutes (this makes the skins steam off and you can peel them more easily). Cut each pepper piece in half again.

Line the loaf tin with clingfilm, then gently press slices of aubergine over the base and sides of the tin. Reserve 4 slices for the top. Spread generously with some of the ricotta mixture, then add a layer of yellow pepper, taking it up the sides of the tin if you can. Sprinkle with some of the basil, then spread with more ricotta mixture. Layer the red pepper next, followed by courgette, adding a layer of the ricotta and basil after each vegetable. Top with the reserved aubergine slices. Cover the top with clingfilm and put a weight on top. Leave overnight in the refrigerator.

Invert the loaf onto a plate and carefully pull away the clingfilm. Using a serrated knife, cut into thick slices, then serve.

2 aubergines, cut lengthways into about 5 slices

olive oil, for brushing

1 red pepper, halved and deseeded

1 yellow pepper, halved and deseeded

2 courgettes, sliced lengthways

250 g ricotta cheese

2 tablespoons freshly squeezed lemon juice

1 garlic clove, crushed

a large handful of flat leaf parsley, finely chopped

1 red chilli, deseeded and finely chopped

1 tablespoon balsamic vinegar

a large handful of fresh basil leaves, torn

sea salt and freshly ground black pepper

2 large baking trays

a loaf tin, 900 g

Serves 6–8

If you can find them, use the baby Asian aubergines to make this dish – they look very pretty and have a more interesting texture than large aubergines.

baked aubergines with pesto

300 g baby aubergines

4 tablespoons olive oil

Pesto

a large bunch of fresh basil

75 g pine nuts, lightly toasted in a dry frying pan

1 garlic clove, peeled

75 g Parmesan cheese, grated

6–8 tablespoons olive oil

sea salt and freshly ground black pepper

a baking tray, lightly oiled

Serves 4

Preheat the oven to 190°C (375°F) Gas 5.

Cut the aubergines in half lengthways and put on the baking tray. Drizzle with a little of the oil and bake in the preheated oven for 15–20 minutes, then turn them over and cook for a further 15 minutes.

To make the pesto, put the basil, pine nuts, garlic, Parmesan, the remaining olive oil and seasoning in a blender and purée until smooth. When the aubergines are cooked, drizzle with pesto and serve hot or cold.

Cook's tip Make twice the quantity of pesto and store the extra in the refrigerator – it always comes in handy as an easy salad dressing or tossed through pasta for a quick, delicious supper. Keep the pesto covered with a thin film of olive oil and it will stay fresh for several weeks.

Made with almonds, basil and tomato, the pesto in this recipe comes from Trapane in Sicily, where it is known as *pesto trapanese*. It is traditionally served with a regional pasta called busiate, which is similar to bucatini. The rich smoky flavour of toasted almonds and the peppery flavour of the basil permeate the risotto rice, making the perfect combination.

risotto
with sicilian pesto

2 shallots, finely chopped

500 g risotto rice, preferably vialone nano

60 ml white wine

1 litre hot vegetable stock

extra virgin olive oil, for frying, plus extra to serve

Sicilian pesto

75 g toasted sliced almonds*, plus extra to serve

80 g fresh basil leaves

4 garlic cloves, lightly crushed

800 g tinned whole plum tomatoes drained, deseeded and chopped

125 ml olive oil

75 g freshly grated pecorino cheese, plus extra to serve

sea salt and freshly ground black pepper

Serves 4

To make the pesto, put the almonds in a food processor with a pinch of salt and grind finely. Transfer to a large bowl.

Put the basil, garlic and tomato in a food processor and reduce to a paste. Add to the ground almonds and stir in the olive oil, pecorino cheese and a good grinding of salt and pepper to taste. Mix well and leave to rest for at least 2 hours.

Cover the base of a large, heavy-based pan with olive oil, heat gently and add the shallots and 2 tablespoons of water. Cook until the shallots are transparent. Add the rice, increase the heat and cook for 2 minutes, stirring continuously. Add the wine and allow it to evaporate, then reduce the heat.

Level the rice and carefully spoon 10 ladles of freshly boiled stock over the rice, cover with a lid and cook over low heat for 15 minutes. After this time, add the pesto and mix energetically for 1 minute. Turn off the heat, cover and leave to stand for 4–5 minutes.

Transfer the risotto to a serving dish or individual plates, then drizzle with olive oil and sprinkle with almond slices. Serve immediately with pecorino cheese.

* If ready-toasted sliced almonds are not available, put untoasted sliced almonds on a heavy baking tray and bake in a preheated oven at 100°C (200°F) Gas Low for 40 minutes or until golden brown. Remove from the sheet and leave to cool before grinding.

8 baby aubergines, left whole

3–4 small courgettes, cut into 4 lengthways

2 red peppers, with stalk and seeds removed, and cut into 4 lengthways

4 garlic cloves, peeled and cut into 4 lengthways

a thumb-sized piece of fresh ginger, peeled and cut into thin sticks

100 ml olive oil

sea salt

a bunch of fresh coriander, coarsely chopped

a bunch of fresh mint, coarsely chopped

Lemon couscous

500 g couscous

1/2 teaspoon sea salt

600 ml warm water

1–2 tablespoons olive oil

1 preserved lemon, finely chopped

15 g unsalted butter

Serves 4

This recipe is a wonderful main course for vegetarians. For a variation, instead of roasting the vegetables, you could prepare vegetable kebabs on the barbecue and serve them with the couscous. Generally, aubergines, courgettes and peppers are roasted together but you can vary the vegetables, according to the season.

lemon couscous
with roasted vegetables

Preheat the oven to 200°C (400°F) Gas 6.

Put the vegetables, garlic and ginger in an ovenproof dish. Pour over the oil, sprinkle with salt and cook in the preheated oven for about 40 minutes, until the vegetables are tender and nicely browned.

To make the lemon couscous, tip the couscous into an ovenproof dish. Stir the salt into the water and pour it over the couscous. Leave it to absorb the water for about 10 minutes. Using your fingers, rub the oil into the couscous grains to break up the lumps and aerate them. Toss in the preserved lemon, scatter the butter over the surface and cover with a piece of aluminium foil or wet greaseproof paper. Put the dish in the oven for about 15 minutes, until the couscous has heated through.

Tip the couscous onto a serving plate in a mound. Arrange the vegetables over and around it and spoon some of the roasting oil over the top. Sprinkle with the coriander and mint and serve immediately.

crab spaghetti
with chilli mussels

This deliciously simple dish can also be made on a barbecue but remember to take two saucepans and a colander outside with you.

7 tablespoons olive oil

1 onion, chopped

2 garlic cloves, crushed and chopped

1 x 400-g tin chopped tomatoes

1 glass white wine, about 150 ml

1 mild red chilli, deseeded and finely chopped

375 g dried spaghetti

400 g cleaned mussels

1 dressed crab

freshly squeezed juice of 1 lemon

fresh flat leaf parsley, coarsely chopped, to serve

sea salt and freshly ground black pepper

Serves 4

Heat 4 tablespoons of the olive oil in a medium saucepan over high heat (or over hot coals, if using a barbecue). Add the onion and garlic and cook until softened and translucent.

Add the tomatoes, white wine, chopped chilli, salt and pepper. Mix well, bring to the boil and simmer for about 10 minutes to reduce and thicken the sauce.

Bring a large saucepan of water to the boil, add the spaghetti and push it down into the water. Stir to separate the strands and stop them sticking together. Cook for about 9 minutes, or until al dente.

Meanwhile, discard any open mussels that will not close when tapped sharply with a knife. Add the mussels to the sauce, mix well, then cover with a lid and simmer for 4 minutes.

Drain the spaghetti in a colander. Add the remaining olive oil to the same pan, and gently stir in the crabmeat, lemon juice and chopped parsley. Add the drained spaghetti, return to the heat and toss well to mix all the ingredients.

Serve the spaghetti in piles with spoonfuls of chilli mussels and sauce on top.

Cook's tips Try to buy a dressed crab, readily available in supermarkets, food halls and from fishmongers by the sea. Cooking a fresh, raw crab is very simple, but extracting the meat can be a long, slow process. With a dressed crab the fiddly work is done for you, and it tastes much better than tinned crab.

If any mussels remain unopened after cooking, it may be that there wasn't enough heat generated in the saucepan. Make sure the pan is boiling and covered. If any of the mussels still don't open, discard them.

stuffed greek aubergines

In Greece, these stuffed aubergines are called *papoutsakias*, which means 'little shoes', and they do, in fact, look like slippers. Traditionally, the dish is flavoured with basil leaves, but oregano has been used here. Don't be shocked by the amounts of garlic and oil, or by the cooking time. Serve with chunks of crusty bread and a robust red wine. Imam bayildi, the great Turkish classic dish, is similar to this recipe.

Preheat the oven to 180°C (350°F) Gas 4.

Using a sharp, serrated knife, cut out the central flesh of the aubergine halves, leaving a 1 cm shell. Cut the flesh into 1 cm chunks. Heat 4 tablespoons of the oil in a large frying pan, add the garlic and aubergine halves cut sides down. Cook over moderate heat for 5 minutes. Remove and set the aubergine halves, cut side up, in a baking dish, ready to be filled. Leave the oil and garlic in the pan.

Put the aubergine halves in the preheated oven for 15 minutes while you prepare the filling and sauce.

Add the aubergine cubes to the oil in the pan. Fry for 5 minutes, then add the onion, tomatoes, celery, if using, and the dried oregano and cook over high heat. Add the remaining oil and cook, stirring constantly, until the aubergine chunks are fairly soft and the tomatoes reduced. Scoop up the aubergine pieces with some of the other vegetables, pile them inside the part-cooked shells and bake them for a further 40 minutes.

Meanwhile, add the tomato purée to the pan, then add 175 ml boiling water. Stir over gentle heat for a further 15 minutes to form a rich, soft, fragrant sauce, then turn off the heat. Taste and season well with salt and pepper.

After 1 hour in the oven, test the aubergines: the outer shells should be dark, wrinkled and soft. If not, cook them for another 20 minutes. Serve the aubergines in their baking dish or a serving plate, with the sauce poured over and around. Top with the fresh herbs and cheese, if using. Serve hot, warm or cool.

2 large aubergines, about 600–700 g, halved lengthways

6 tablespoons extra virgin olive oil

6 garlic cloves, crushed

1 red or white onion, sliced into rings

6 firm-fleshed ripe red tomatoes, blanched, skinned, then cut into segments

2 celery stalks (optional)

1 teaspoon dried oregano

4 tablespoons thick tomato purée

sprigs of fresh oregano, marjoram or thyme (optional)

4 thin slices cheese, such as Greek kasseri, Cheddar or pecorino, about 50 g (optional)

sea salt and freshly ground black pepper

a baking dish big enough to hold the aubergines in a single layer

Serves 4

easy fish stew

This easy, stress-free recipe makes a fantastic meal. Don't forget to provide a few empty dishes for discarded shells and some bowls of warm water for washing fingers.

5 tablespoons olive oil

3 garlic cloves, chopped

2 onions, chopped

2 leeks, trimmed and sliced

3 celery stalks, sliced

1 fennel bulb, trimmed and sliced

1 tablespoon plain flour

1 bay leaf

a sprig of fresh thyme

a generous pinch of saffron threads

3 x 400-g tins chopped tomatoes

2 litres fish stock

1 kg monkfish tail, cut into 8

500 g mussels in shells, scrubbed

8 scallops

8 uncooked prawns, shell on

a bunch of fresh flat leaf parsley, chopped

sea salt and freshly ground black pepper

Serves 8

Heat the oil in a large saucepan and add the garlic, onion, leeks, celery and fennel. Cook over low to medium heat for 10 minutes until soft. Sprinkle in the flour and stir well. Add the bay leaf, thyme, saffron, tomatoes, fish stock and salt and pepper to taste. Bring to the boil, then simmer for 25 minutes.

Add the monkfish, mussels, scallops and prawns, cover with a lid and simmer very gently for 6 minutes. Remove from the heat and set aside, with the lid on, for 4 minutes. Add the parsley and serve with plenty of warm crusty bread.

prawn noodle broth

If you love a fiery heat, leave the seeds in the chillies.

Heat the oil in a saucepan and add the onion, ginger, garlic and chillies. Stir well and cook for 5 minutes over low heat. Add the prawns and cook for a further 2 minutes, then add the stock. Bring to the boil, add the noodles and cook for a further 2 minutes. Stir the Thai basil and coriander into the broth and serve.

1 tablespoon vegetable oil

1 onion, sliced

10 cm fresh ginger, peeled and sliced

2 garlic cloves, sliced

2 red chillies, deseeded (optional) and sliced

600 g uncooked shelled tiger prawns

2 litres vegetable stock

600 g fresh udon noodles

a bunch of fresh Thai basil, coarsely chopped

a bunch of fresh coriander, coarsely chopped

Serves 8

sicilian-spiced seabass
with grilled tomatoes and baby fennel

Perfect for a barbecue, this simple dish can be cooked outdoors at the tableside. Ask your fishmonger to gut and descale the seabass for you, but if whole fish doesn't appeal, replace the seabass with tuna or swordfish steaks.

Preheat the barbecue.

Crush the fennel seeds, oregano, cumin seeds, salt, peppercorns and chilli together thoroughly using a pestle and mortar. Make 3 slashes in each side of the fish with a sharp knife. Brush olive oil all over the fish and rub the pounded spices over it and into the slits. Cut 2 of the lemons in half vertically, then cut 1½ into thin slices. Cut or tear the bay leaves into halves or thirds. Place half a slice of lemon and a piece of bay leaf in each slit. Cut each fennel bulb in quarters lengthways and thread the cherry tomatoes onto the skewers. Brush the fish, fennel and tomatoes with oil and grill over medium heat until charred, turning them halfway through, removing them as they are cooked. Serve with wedges of lemon.

Cook's tip You could cook the fish under a conventional grill instead or, in the case of tuna and swordfish, in a non-stick frying pan.

1 rounded teaspoon fennel seeds

1 rounded teaspoon dried oregano

1 teaspoon cumin seeds

1 teaspoon sea salt

1 teaspoon green or black peppercorns

¼ teaspoon crushed chillies

6 small seabass, gutted and scaled

extra virgin olive oil, to brush

3 unwaxed lemons

a few bay leaves

4 baby fennel bulbs

350 g cherry tomatoes

wedges of lemon, to serve

6 wooden skewers, soaked in water for 30 minutes

Serves 6

1 whole trout, about 2 kg, filleted and skinned

12 slices prosciutto

2 tablespoons toasted sesame oil

Cucumber salad

2 cucumbers, peeled and halved lengthways

grated zest and freshly squeezed juice of 2 unwaxed limes

sea salt and freshly ground black pepper

an old roasting tin, lined with foil

75 g oak wood shavings

1 tablespoon jasmine tea leaves

a wire rack

Serves 8

tea-smoked trout with cucumber salad

This unusual treat for the taste buds takes a little time to make, but for that special occasion it is well worth it.

Put the wood shavings and tea into the lined roasting tin and mix well. Put a wire rack that fits the tin on top.

Put both trout fillets onto a cutting board, one on top of the other, top to tail. Shape with your hands into a long sausage. Wrap the prosciutto around the fillets, overlapping slightly, to cover completely. Tie pieces of kitchen string around the trout at 5 cm intervals to secure, then cut into 8 thick slices. Rub the cut surfaces with sesame oil and transfer to the wire rack set over the roasting tin.

Completely cover the top of the tin with foil, making sure that it is sealed all the way around the edge to stop any smoke escaping. Put the tin over high heat on the hob for 10 minutes, moving it around from time to time, to ensure even smoking.

Remove from the heat and leave to cool, covered, for 20 minutes.

To make the cucumber salad, scoop out the seeds from the peeled cucumber halves and discard. Finely slice the cucumber and put into a bowl. Add the lime zest and juice and salt and pepper to taste.

Heat a ridged stove-top grill pan or a non-stick frying pan until hot, add the smoked trout steaks and cook for 3 minutes on each side. They should be brown and slightly crunchy on the outside.

Remove and discard the string and serve the fish with the cucumber salad.

This simple but tasty dish can equally well be adapted to a conventional grill or a barbecue. You would then need to fry the tomatoes quickly in a frying pan to serve with the salad.

seared tuna
with tomatoes, rocket and gremolata

To make the gremolata, grate the zest finely from the lemons, taking care not to remove too much white pith. Take the tough ends off the parsley stalks and finely chop the leaves. Roughly chop the capers, then pull all the ingredients together with the garlic on the chopping board and chop them together to mix them thoroughly. Set aside in a bowl. Quarter the lemons.

When you're ready to cook, heat a ridged stove-top grill pan or frying pan until almost smoking (about 3 minutes). Rub both sides

of the tuna steaks with olive oil and season with sea salt rubbed between your fingers and black pepper. Lay as many tuna steaks as you can fit in the pan and cook for about 1½–2 minutes, depending on the thickness and how rare you like them. Turn them over and cook the other side for 1–1½ minutes. Set aside on a warmed serving dish and cover lightly with foil. Repeat with the remaining tuna steaks.

Rinse the pan under hot running water, dry with kitchen paper and reheat until very hot. Add 2 tablespoons olive oil and tip in the tomatoes. Cook for 1–1½ minutes, shaking the pan until the skins start to split, then turn off the heat.

To serve, put a small handful of rocket on each plate, top with a few tomatoes and lay the tuna steaks alongside. Drizzle the tuna and salad with olive oil and a good squeeze of lemon juice, and sprinkle over the gremolata. Serve with some authentic French crusty baguette.

6 fresh tuna steaks, about 150 g each

350 g pomodorino or other cherry tomatoes

100 g wild rocket

sea salt and freshly ground black pepper

extra virgin olive oil, to drizzle

Gremolata

2 unwaxed lemons

40 g fresh fresh flat leaf parsley

2 rounded tablespoons capers, rinsed if salted

3 large garlic cloves, finely chopped

Serves 6

orange and soy-glazed duck

4 duck breast fillets, about 250 g each

freshly squeezed juice of 1 orange

3 tablespoons dark soy sauce

2 tablespoons maple syrup

1/2 teaspoon Chinese five-spice powder

2 garlic cloves, crushed

freshly ground Szechuan peppercorns or black pepper

steamed broccoli or pak-choi, or sautéed spinach, to serve

1 orange, cut into wedges, to serve

Serves 4

This is a great dish when you are short of time – it is quick to cook and tastes delicious. Serve the duck breasts with your choice of vegetables such as steamed pak-choi, steamed broccoli or sautéed spinach.

Using a sharp knife, score the fat on each duck breast crossways several times. Put the breasts into a shallow dish.

Put the orange juice, soy sauce, maple syrup, Chinese five-spice powder, garlic and pepper into a small jug or bowl, mix well, then pour the mixture over the fillets. Cover with clingfilm and marinate in the refrigerator for as long as possible. You can leave them overnight, but return them to room temperature for 1 hour before cooking.

Preheat the oven to 200°C (400°F) Gas 6.

Heat a ridged stove-top grill pan until hot, add the duck breasts, skin side down, and sear for 1–2 minutes. Transfer to a roasting tin, adding the marinade juices. Cook the duck in the preheated oven for about 10 minutes or until medium rare. Remove the duck from the oven, wrap it in foil and keep it warm for 5 minutes.

Pour the juices from the roasting tin into a small saucepan and, using a large spoon, very carefully skim the fat off the surface. Transfer the pan to the top of the stove and bring the juices to the boil for 2 minutes, until thickened slightly. Serve the duck breasts sprinkled with the juices and accompanied by broccoli, pak-choi or spinach and wedges of orange.

chicken and tarragon pesto pasta

Pesto can be made out of most herbs, so don't hesitate to try your favourites and make your own blend for this recipe. If you like, replace the chicken with steamed vegetables such as courgettes, sugar snap peas, broad beans or runner beans.

300 g dried penne pasta

9 tablespoons olive oil

75 g Parmesan cheese, freshly grated

75 g pine nuts, toasted in a dry frying pan

a large bunch of tarragon, leaves stripped from the stem and chopped

grated zest and freshly squeezed juice of 1 unwaxed lemon

1 garlic clove, chopped

3 cooked chicken breasts, sliced

100 g rocket

sea salt and freshly ground black pepper

Serves 4

Bring a large saucepan of water to the boil. Add the pasta, stir and cook for 8–9 minutes, until al dente. When cooked, drain and refresh the pasta in cold water, then drain thoroughly and toss in 4 tablespoons of the oil.

To make the pesto, put the Parmesan, pine nuts, tarragon, lemon zest and juice, garlic and remaining oil in a jug and purée until smooth with a hand-held blender.

Put the pasta, pesto, chicken and rocket in a serving bowl, season and toss well, coating the pasta and chicken evenly with the pesto.

Cook's tip When taking this salad on a picnic, don't add the rocket until just before eating or the oil will make it wilt.

Stuffed with aromatic, fruity couscous, this dish is really a meal on its own, accompanied by a salad.

roast chicken
stuffed with couscous, apricots and dates

2 garlic cloves, crushed

2 teaspoons dried oregano or thyme

1–2 teaspoons paprika

2 tablespoons salted butter, softened

1 large organic chicken, about 1.5 kg

1 sliced-off orange end

150 ml chicken stock

Couscous stuffing

225 g couscous

1/2 teaspoon salt

225 ml warm water

1 tablespoon olive oil

1–2 teaspoons ground cinnamon

1 teaspoon ground coriander

1/2 teaspoon ground cumin

1 tablespoon clear honey

2 tablespoons golden raisins

125 g ready-to-eat dried apricots, thickly sliced

125 g ready-to-eat dates, thickly sliced or chopped

2–3 tablespoons blanched almonds, roasted

Serves 4–6

Preheat the oven to 180°C (350°F) Gas 4.

To make the couscous stuffing, tip the couscous into a large bowl. Stir the salt into the warm water and pour it over the couscous, stirring all the time so that the water is absorbed evenly. Leave the couscous to swell for about 10 minutes then, using your fingers, rub the oil into the couscous to break up the lumps and aerate it. Stir in the other stuffing ingredients and set aside.

In a small bowl, beat the garlic, oregano and paprika into the softened butter then smear it all over the chicken, inside and out. Put the chicken in the base of a tagine or in an ovenproof dish and fill the cavity with as much of the couscous stuffing as you can (any leftover couscous can be heated through in the oven before serving and fluffed up with a little extra oil or butter). Seal the cavity with the slice of orange (you can squeeze the juice from the rest of the orange over the chicken). Pour the stock into the base of the tagine and roast the chicken in the oven for 1–1½ hours, basting from time to time, until the chicken is cooked.

Remove the chicken from the oven and leave to rest for 10 minutes before carving or jointing it and strain the cooking juices into a jug. Heat up any remaining couscous (as described above) and serve with the chicken, the jug of cooking juices to pour over and a green salad.

rosemary and lemon roasted chicken

For simple dishes such as this, quality ingredients are important. Choose an organic chicken, unwaxed lemons, a good Modena balsamic vinegar and extra virgin olive oil.

about 2 kg chicken pieces, or 1 whole chicken*

3 lemons, cut into wedges

leaves from a large bunch of fresh rosemary

3 red onions

75 g large black olives, about 10–12, stoned

4 tablespoons balsamic vinegar

2 tablespoons extra virgin olive oil

sea salt and freshly ground black pepper

Serves 4

Trim off any excess fat from the chicken pieces and put them in a large bowl. Add the lemon and rosemary.

Cut the onions in half lengthways, leaving the root end intact. Cut the halves into wedges and add to the chicken.

Add the olives, balsamic vinegar, olive oil and seasoning and mix well to coat the chicken with the flavourings.

Cover and leave to stand at room temperature for 1 hour, or in the refrigerator overnight.

Preheat the oven to 190°C (375°F) Gas 5.

Put the chicken in a large roasting tin, then add the marinade ingredients. Cook in the preheated oven for 30 minutes. Turn the chicken pieces thoroughly in the tin to ensure even cooking and colouring, then cook for a further 30 minutes.

Remove the chicken from the oven. Using a slotted spoon, lift out the chicken, lemon, onions and olives and put them on a serving dish.

Skim the cooking juices, discarding the fat. Pour the juices over the chicken and serve hot or at room temperature.

* If using a whole chicken, lay the bird on its back. Use a large knife to cut through the skin between the leg and breast of the chicken, then bend the leg backwards until the joint cracks. Cut through the joint to separate the leg. Repeat on the other side.

Bend the drumsticks back away from the thighs to crack the joints, then cut through with the knife to separate. Bend back the wings of the chicken and cut through the joints near each breast to separate.

Put the bird on its side and use scissors or poultry shears to cut from the leg joint up along the backbone to the neck. Repeat along the other side. (Wrap the backbone and store for use in stock another day.)

Hold the chicken breast-side down and bend it back to crack the breastbone. Use the scissors to cut along each side of the breastbone and remove the breasts.

korean chicken

Remove any excess fat from the chicken pieces and drain off the oil while cooking.

2 kg chicken pieces, trimmed

4 tablespoons toasted sesame oil

100 ml light soy sauce

4 garlic cloves, very finely chopped

1 teaspoon chilli powder

5 spring onions, very finely chopped

freshly ground black pepper

500 g dried egg noodles, to serve

1 teaspoon black sesame seeds (optional), to serve

Serves 8

Put the chicken into an ovenproof dish, add the sesame oil, soy sauce, garlic, chilli powder, spring onions and black pepper to taste. Mix well, cover and chill overnight.

Preheat the oven to 180°C (350°F) Gas 4. Uncover the chicken and cook in the preheated oven for 30 minutes. Reduce to 140°C (275°F) Gas 1 and cook for a further 40 minutes. Meanwhile, cook the noodles according to the directions on the packet. Drain, then serve the chicken and noodles, sprinkled with the black sesame seeds, if using.

chicken sauté provence-style

In the Vaucluse area of Provence, tomatoes are nicknamed *pommes d'amour* – love apples – and this dish of pan-cooked chicken, which includes lots of them, certainly inspires affection. It might once have been made outdoors, over a wood fire. If possible, try to use a youngish chicken, ideally one raised in the open, its diet enriched by corn, for the most characterful results.

Pat dry the chicken pieces and rub all over with salt and pepper. Heat the oil in a very large, heavy-based frying pan or a flameproof casserole. Fry half the chicken over high heat for 10 minutes, pressing the pieces down hard for maximum contact with the pan, and turning them often until golden brown. Transfer the chicken to a plate, and cook the second batch in the same way. Set aside with the first lot.

Put the onion in the pan and fry for 1 minute, stirring. Pour in the wine and add the bouquet garni, scraping up the sediment as the wine reduces by half. Add the tomatoes, tomato purée and olives, and cook for 3–5 minutes over high heat, stirring. Return the chicken to the pan, cover with foil or a lid and cook for 8–10 minutes, or until very tender.

Mix the garlic and parsley together, then scatter this topping over the chicken and serve hot.

a 1.5-kg frying chicken, cut into 10 or 12 pieces

4 tablespoons extra virgin olive oil

1 onion, sliced

100 ml medium-dry white or rosé wine

1 fresh bouquet garni: oregano, marjoram, bay and basil

350 g ripe, flavoursome tomatoes, peeled and chopped

2 tablespoons tomato purée

12 stoned, salt-cured black olives, lightly crushed

4 garlic cloves, finely chopped

a small handful of fresh flat leaf parsley, finely chopped, or a mixture of fresh herbs

salt and freshly ground black pepper

Serves 4–6

These individual meat pies are a little tricky to make, but if you follow the cooking method carefully, after you have made the first one, the rest is plain sailing. They make terrific picnic food and are far better than shop-bought pies.

mini pork and apple pies

250 g pork fillet, diced

125 g pork belly, diced

75 g smoked bacon, diced

25 g chicken livers

1 small onion, minced

1 tablespoon chopped fresh sage

1 small garlic clove, crushed

a pinch of ground nutmeg

1 red apple, peeled, cored and diced

sea salt and freshly ground black pepper

Pastry

300 g plain flour, plus extra for kneading

1½ teaspoons salt

60 g white vegetable fat

Glaze

1 egg yolk

1 tablespoon milk

6 pieces of wax paper, about 30 x 7 cm

Serves 6

Preheat the oven to 190°C (375°F) Gas 5.

Put the pork fillet, pork belly, bacon and chicken livers into a food processor and blend briefly to mince the meat. Transfer to a bowl and mix in the onion, sage, garlic, nutmeg and a little salt and pepper. Set aside.

To make the pastry, sift the flour and salt into a bowl. Put the fat and 150 ml water into a saucepan and heat gently until the fat

melts and the water comes to the boil. Pour the liquid into the flour and, using a wooden spoon, gently draw the flour into the liquid to form a soft dough.

Leave to cool for a few minutes and, as soon as the dough is cool enough to handle, knead lightly in the bowl until smooth.

Divide the dough into 8 and roll out 6 of these on a lightly floured surface to form discs 12 cm across. Carefully invert them, one at a time, over an upturned jam jar. Wrap a piece of waxed paper around the outside, then tie around the middle with kitchen string.

Turn the whole thing over so the pastry is sitting flat. Carefully work the jar up and out of the pastry shell (you may need to slip a small palette knife down between the pastry and the jar, to loosen it).

Divide the pork filling into 6 portions and put 1 portion into each pie. Put the diced apple on top. Roll out the remaining 2 pieces of dough and cut 3 rounds from each piece with a pastry cutter, the same size as the top of the pies.

Put a pastry round on top of each pie, press the edges together to seal, then turn the edges inwards and over to form a rim.

To make the glaze, put the egg yolk and milk into a bowl, beat well, then brush over the tops of the pies. Pierce each one with a fork to allow the steam to escape.

Transfer to a large baking tray and cook in the preheated oven for 45–50 minutes until golden. Remove from the oven, transfer to a wire rack, leave to cool and serve cold with a green salad.

sage-stuffed pork fillet
with puy lentils and spring onion dressing

This very simple but impressive dish would suit a smart outdoor lunch. Fillet of pork is a much under-used cut, but it is so quick and easy to cook. If you follow these instructions, you can rest assured that it will be cooked through and moist.

Preheat the oven to 180°C (350°F) Gas 4.

Trim the pork fillets of any excess fat and, using a long, thin knife, pierce each fillet lengthways through the middle. Push the sage leaves into the slit and, using the handle of a wooden spoon, push them further along the slit. Sprinkle the fillets with salt and pepper, then wrap each one in 4 slices of Parma ham. Brush a roasting tin with oil, add the wrapped fillets and cook in the preheated oven for 35 minutes. Remove, leave to rest for 5 minutes, then cut into 3 cm thick slices.

Meanwhile, cook the lentils in simmering water for 20 minutes until tender, then drain. Put the spring onions into a bowl, add the olive oil, wine and soured cream and mix. Add the peppers to the drained lentils and spoon onto serving plates. Top with the pork slices, spring onion dressing and chives, then serve.

2 pork fillets, about 375 g each

leaves from a large bunch of fresh sage

8 thin slices Parma ham

250 g Puy lentils

6 spring onions, sliced

3 tablespoons olive oil

1 tablespoon red wine

100 ml soured cream

500 g roasted red peppers in a jar, drained and cut into strips

a bunch of fresh chives, snipped

sea salt and freshly ground black pepper

a large roasting tin

Serves 8

The blue cheese butter is a strongly flavoured and delicious topping for the fillet steak. A simple salad of baby spinach is the only accompaniment you'll need.

steak
with blue cheese butter

4 fillet steaks, 200 g each

sea salt and freshly ground black pepper

baby spinach salad, to serve

Blue cheese butter

50 g unsalted butter, softened

50 g soft blue cheese, such as Gorgonzola

25 g shelled walnuts, finely ground in a blender

2 tablespoons chopped fresh parsley

sea salt and freshly ground black pepper

Serves 4

To make the blue cheese butter, put the butter, cheese, walnuts and parsley into a bowl and beat well. Season to taste. Form into a log, wrap in aluminium foil and chill for about 30 minutes.

Preheat the barbecue.

Lightly season the steaks and cook on the preheated barbecue (or pan-fry in a little oil) for 3 minutes on each side for rare, or 4–5 minutes for medium to well done.

Cut the butter into 8 slices. Put 2 slices of butter onto each cooked steak, wrap loosely with foil and leave to rest for 5 minutes.

Serve with a salad of baby spinach.

desserts

peaches in rose syrup

Voluptuous, blushy-pink peaches in a syrup of flower-scented rosé wine are a wonderfully indulgent dessert. In the South of France, where this dessert comes from, the peaches are served with *calissons d'Aix* – eye-shaped candied sweetmeats sold in lozenge-shaped boxes. Almonds, candied melon and boiled honey syrup go into the mix, as do candied orange, mandarin and apricot. Rice paper bases and snowy white icing complete the picture. These, with the poached peaches and rose petal decoration, create a blissful dessert. The *calissons* are hard to find outside France, so you can just serve the dessert with some delicate sweet wafers instead, if you like.

4 large, ripe peaches, ideally white-fleshed

400 ml medium-sweet rosé wine

75 g clear wildflower honey

1 teaspoon rosewater

75 ml *marc* (*eau de vie*)

16 sugared rose petals or fresh pink rose petals, to serve (optional)

Serves 4

Rub the fuzzy layer from the peach skin. Make a criss-cross cut at the stalk end and the base of each peach.

Put the wine, honey and rosewater in a deep, medium saucepan big enough to hold the peaches in a single layer. Bring this liquid to the boil.

Add the peaches and reduce the heat to a lively simmer. Splash the syrup all over the peaches as they cook, and tilt the pan to rotate them and ensure even cooking. Try to avoid stirring. Cook for a minimum of 6–8 minutes.

Using a slotted spoon, transfer the peaches, one by one, to a plate. Pull off and discard the skin, then leave the fruit to cool completely.

Leave the wine syrup to cool, then stir in the marc.

To serve, put each peach into a bowl. Drizzle over the syrup and scatter the petals on top (if using).

pan-grilled strawberries
with black pepper ice cream

Strawberries and black pepper are an unusual but famous food combination that works really
well. Strawberries with ice cream is also a match made in heaven, so why not combine the two ideas?
The slight heat from the pepper hits the taste buds last and marries beautifully with the sweet fruit.

10 g unsalted butter

250 g strawberries, left whole with green stalks

icing sugar, for sprinkling

Pepper ice cream

100 g caster sugar

125 g mascarpone cheese

125 g Greek yoghurt

2 level teaspoons freshly ground black pepper

an ice-cream maker or freezer-proof container

Serves 4

To make the ice cream, put the sugar and 250 ml water in a small saucepan and set over
gentle heat until the sugar has dissolved. Leave to cool. Put the mascarpone, yoghurt and
black pepper in a bowl and beat well. Using a hand whisk, beat the creamy mixture into the
cooled sweet liquid.

Transfer to an ice-cream maker and continue according to the manufacturer's instructions.
Alternatively, transfer into a rigid container and freeze for 1½–2 hours, or until the mixture
has set about 3 cm from the edge. Whisk to break down the larger crystals, then return to the
freezer for 4 hours or overnight. Remove from the freezer 15 minutes before serving to soften.

To cook the strawberries, heat a ridged stove-top grill pan until smoking hot. Add the butter
and, when melted, add the strawberries. Press lightly onto the pan so they are branded with
black lines. Turn them over and do the same on the other side. Serve immediately, dusted
with icing sugar accompanied by a scoop of black pepper ice cream.

Cook's tip Do not overcook the strawberries – the idea is that they remain firm with only
the outsides slightly softened by the heat.

75 g icing sugar, sifted

175 g unsalted butter, at room temperature

2 egg yolks

30 ml (2 tablespoons) iced water

250 g plain flour, sifted

Lemon filling

4 eggs

150 g caster sugar

2 tablespoons grated lemon zest and 125 ml freshly squeezed lemon juice from 2–3 unwaxed lemons

100 ml double cream, plus extra to serve

a shallow, loose-bottomed 20 cm tart tin, no more than 3 cm deep, set on a baking tray

greaseproof paper and baking beans

Serves 4

Lemon tart – wobbly, sharp, creamy but acidic – is an outrageously delicious dish. In France, these are often slim, very elegant offerings, not heavily filled. Ideally, make the tart a few hours before you intend to eat it, then serve it warm or cool. Some ice-cold scoops of thick, sharp crème fraîche are the perfect accompaniment. Serve with a small glass of citrus liqueur, dark rum or brandy.

french lemon tart

Set aside 2 tablespoons of the icing sugar and put the remainder in the bowl of an electric mixer. Add the butter and beat until creamy, soft and white. Add the egg yolks one at a time and continue beating until well mixed. Trickle in half the iced water, then add the flour. Whisk on a lower speed, adding the remaining water until the pastry gathers into a soft ball. Wrap in clingfilm, and chill for 40–60 minutes.

Preheat the oven to 180°C (350°F) Gas 4.

Transfer the pastry to a floured work surface and roll out to 5 mm thick. Use it to line the tart tin. Gently push the dough into the corners. Cut off the excess pastry. Chill for a further 20 minutes or until very firm.

Prick the pastry all over with a fork, line with greaseproof paper, fill with baking beans and bake blind in the preheated oven for 15 minutes. Remove the paper and the beans. Leave the pastry to rest for 5 minutes, then bake again for 10 minutes or until pale golden. Cut off any excess pastry to make a neat edge.

Lower the oven temperature to 120°C (250°F) Gas ½.

To make the filling, put the eggs, sugar and half the lemon zest in a bowl and beat well for 2 minutes with an electric whisk. Stir in the lemon juice and cream, then pour the mixture into the tart shell. Bake for 35 minutes, or until the filling is barely set.

While the tart cooks, put the remaining lemon zest in a sieve, pour over boiling water, then refresh under cold running water. Put the zest, the reserved 2 tablespoons icing sugar and 4 tablespoons water in a saucepan over low heat. Cook gently until the zest looks syrupy. Sprinkle the zest over the cooked tart. Serve hot or warm, with additional spoonfuls of cream.

This freshly baked, moist yet crumbly aromatic pineapple loaf needs no more than a dusting of icing sugar on top. When taking a cake on a picnic, don't forget to put a knife in the tin.

pineapple and thyme loaf cake

150 g unsalted butter or margarine

150 g caster sugar

3 eggs, beaten

75 g self-raising flour

75 g semolina

2 teaspoons baking powder

250 g tinned pineapple chunks, chopped in a food processor

1 tablespoon finely chopped fresh thyme

15 g vanilla sugar (page 145) or 1 teaspoon vanilla extract

icing sugar, to dust (optional)

a loaf tin, 1 kg, lined with greaseproof paper

Serves 8

Preheat the oven to 190°C (375°F) Gas 5.

Put the butter and sugar in a large mixing bowl and beat until light and fluffy. Add the eggs a little at a time, beating well after each addition; it may be necessary to add a little of the flour to prevent the mixture curdling. Fold in the remaining flour, semolina, baking powder, pineapple, thyme and vanilla sugar.

Bake in the preheated oven for 30 minutes or until well risen and golden. When the cake is cool enough to handle, turn out onto a cooling rack and leave to cool. Dust with icing sugar, then wrap in aluminium foil and transfer to a tin.

Wrapping fruits in foil is a great way to cook them on the barbecue – all the juices are contained in the parcel while the fruit softens.

grilled fruit parcels

Preheat the barbecue.

Put the fruit into a large bowl, add the orange juice, cinnamon and sugar and mix well. Divide the fruit mixture between 4 sheets of foil. Fold the foil over the fruit and seal the edges to make parcels.

Put the yoghurt, honey and rosewater into a separate bowl and mix well. Set aside.

Cook the parcels over medium-hot coals for 5–6 minutes. Remove the parcels from the heat, open carefully and transfer to 4 serving bowls. Serve with the yoghurt and a sprinkling of pistachio nuts.

4 peaches or nectarines, halved, stoned and sliced

200 g blueberries

125 g raspberries

freshly squeezed juice of 1 orange

1 teaspoon ground cinnamon

2 tablespoons caster sugar

200 g natural yoghurt

1 tablespoon clear honey

1 tablespoon rosewater

1 tablespoon chopped pistachio nuts

Serves 4

nectarine tart

Crumbly sweet pastry and oozingly juicy nectarines make a sensational combination. The delicate summer flavours of white peaches and apricots make a lovely alternative filling for this tart. Come autumn, don't hesitate to use plums.

Put the flour, butter and icing sugar in a food processor and whizz until the mixture looks like breadcrumbs.

Add the egg yolks and blend the mixture again, just until it comes together to form a ball of dough.

Wrap the pastry in clingfilm and chill in the refrigerator for at least 30 minutes.

Knead the pastry briefly to soften, then on a lightly floured work surface, roll out the pastry into a large circle at least 5 cm wider than the base of the tart tin.

Drape the pastry over the rolling pin, lift it up carefully and lay it over the top of the tin.

Gently press the pastry into the tin, making sure there are no air pockets, then use a sharp knife to trim off the excess pastry. Chill the tart case for 15 minutes.

Preheat the oven to 190°C (375°F) Gas 5.

Cut the nectarines in half, twist to remove the stone, then cut the fruit into slices.

Remove the pastry case from the refrigerator and, working from the outside, arrange the nectarine slices in circles on the pastry, until all the fruit has been used.

Bake in the preheated oven for 30 minutes, then lower the heat to 150°C (300°F) Gas 2 and continue cooking for a further 40 minutes until the fruit is tender and golden and the pastry is crisp.

Dust the tart all over with icing sugar, then serve hot or cold with scoops of good-quality vanilla ice cream.

Cook's tips This pastry is very fragile, but don't despair. Just line your tart tin as best you can, and then add extra pieces of pastry to patch up any cracks or holes.

Instead of serving with vanilla ice cream, you could use Greek yoghurt drizzled with honey; clotted cream; crème fraîche or sweetened fromage frais.

240 g plain flour

250 g unsalted butter, softened and cut into small pieces

100 g icing sugar, plus extra for dusting

2–3 egg yolks

1.25 kg nectarines or peaches

good-quality vanilla ice cream, to serve

a 20 cm loose-bottomed tart tin

Serves 6–8

This wonderful and unusual salad can be served as part of a savoury spread, as an accompaniment to barbecued prawns or as a pudding.

indonesian chilli fruit salad

1/2 ripe pineapple

1 ripe papaya or mango

1 pomelo or pink grapefruit

2 large bananas

2 green apples

Chilli dressing

50 g dark palm sugar or soft brown sugar, about 4 tablespoons

4 tablespoons freshly squeezed lemon juice

2 tablespoons soy sauce

1–2 red chillies, such as serrano, deseeded and finely chopped

Serves 6

To make the dressing, put the sugar, lemon juice, soy sauce and 2 tablespoons water into a small saucepan and heat over a low heat until the sugar has dissolved. Remove from the heat, add the chillies and leave to cool.

Peel, core and cut the pineapple into wedges, then chunks. Peel, deseed and dice the papaya or mango. Peel the pomelo or grapefruit, cut out the segments, and cut each segment in half. Peel and slice the bananas. Peel, core and dice the apples.

Arrange all the fruits in a large bowl, toss gently in the dressing, then chill for about 15 minutes before serving.

summer brioche pudding

Frozen berries work just as well as fresh fruit in this delicious pudding, which means that it can be enjoyed all year round.

4 small individual brioches

500 g fresh or frozen and thawed summer berries

4 tablespoons caster sugar

clotted cream or thick whipped cream, to serve

Serves 4

Carefully trim the tops off the brioches and reserve as the lids. Using a small sharp knife, cut out a large cavity in the middle of each brioche.

Put the fruit and sugar in a saucepan and heat gently until the sugar has dissolved. Dip the brioche lids into the liquid, then start spooning the fruit into the cavity. (It looks like a lot but the brioche will soak up all the fruit and juices.) Put the lids on top at a jaunty angle and chill in the refrigerator for at least 3 hours.

Serve with cream.

This lightly sweetened and spiced cake, known as *buccellato* in its native Lucca in Italy, was traditionally made for every christening. These days, it is sometimes served as a dessert – slices are soaked in Vin Santo and covered with strawberries – but it is also delicious toasted for breakfast.

raisin and aniseed cake

20 g fresh yeast

150 ml milk, warmed

400 g plain white flour, plus extra for dusting

115 g caster sugar

2 eggs, beaten, plus an extra egg white to glaze

50 ml Vin Santo or Marsala

50 g unsalted butter, melted

finely grated zest of 1 unwaxed lemon

1 teaspoon aniseed

50 g raisins

sea salt

a 20 cm ring mould

Makes one 20 cm cake

Mix the yeast with the warm milk until dissolved then allow to stand. Sift the flour into a bowl and mix with the sugar and a pinch of salt. Make a well in the centre and add the yeast mixture, eggs, Vin Santo, melted butter, lemon zest and aniseed. Mix together with a round-bladed knife until the dough begins to come together. The dough should be very soft. Turn out onto a floured surface and knead for 10 minutes until smooth and elastic. Knead in the raisins. Roll into a long sausage and place in the base of the ring mould, pushing the ends together. Cover with a damp tea towel and leave to rise in a warm place for 1½ hours until it doubles in size.

Preheat the oven to 180°C (350°F) Gas 4.

Beat the egg white with a little salt until loose. Uncover the cake and brush the top with the glaze. Bake in the preheated oven for 45 minutes or until risen and deep golden brown. Leave to cool in the tin and when just warm, turn out and cool.

strawberry tart

When any fruit is abundant and in season, it just has to be used in a tart with sweet and crumbling pastry. This combination of wild and farmed strawberries is simply delicious – the tiny wild strawberries look so beautiful and are packed with flavour. If you can't find wild berries, use the same weight in farmed. Any other berries can be used but make sure you pile the tart high.

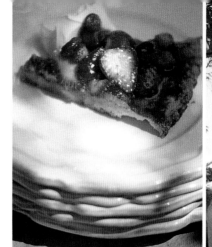

300 g plain flour

200 g butter, cut into small pieces

150 g light brown sugar

2–3 egg yolks, beaten

200 g redcurrant jelly

250 g wild strawberries

750 g farmed strawberries, hulls removed

double cream or Greek yoghurt mixed with clear honey, to serve

a non-stick flan tin, 30 cm diameter

Serves 8

Put the flour into a mixing bowl and add the butter. Using your fingertips, rub the butter into the flour until it looks like breadcrumbs. Add the sugar and mix. Make a well in the middle and add 2 of the egg yolks. Mix with a round-bladed knife, using cutting motions, until the mixture forms a ball, adding an extra egg yolk if needed. Dust your hands lightly with flour, bring the mixture together and transfer to a lightly floured, cool surface.

Preheat the oven to 180°C (350°F) Gas 4.

Roll out the pastry to just bigger than the tin. Line the tin with the pastry, prick all over with a fork and chill for 20 minutes. Cook in the preheated oven for 20 minutes, then lower the heat to 150°C (300°F) Gas 2 and cook for a further 20 minutes. Remove from the oven and leave to cool, then transfer to a flat serving plate and cover with clingfilm until needed.

Put the redcurrant jelly into a small saucepan and heat gently until thin and smooth. Remove and set aside to cool a little while you pile the strawberries into the cooked pastry case, cutting any very large berries into smaller pieces. Spoon the redcurrant jelly over the strawberries and serve with cream or Greek yoghurt mixed with honey.

Preheat the oven to 180°C (350°F) Gas 4.

Put the eggs, sugar, coconut, butter, ground almonds, lemon and orange zest and juice, milk and flour into a food processor and process for 1 minute until blended. Transfer the mixture to the prepared dish and bake in the preheated oven for 45 minutes until golden brown. Remove from the oven and leave to cool.

Put the yoghurt into a bowl and add the mint. Mix well and serve spooned over the bake.

This is simply a sublime dessert – sponge pudding, coconut, ground almonds and citrus fruits.

orange and lemon bake
with minted yoghurt

4 eggs

100 g caster sugar

100 g desiccated coconut

50 g unsalted butter, softened

100 g ground almonds

grated zest and freshly squeezed juice of 2 unwaxed lemons

grated zest and juice of 2 oranges

100 ml milk

50 g self-raising flour

Minted yoghurt

200 ml Greek yoghurt

a bunch of mint, finely chopped

a pie dish, 18 cm in diameter, greased

Serves 8

In this recipe, palm sugar adds the most wonderful toffee flavour to the ice cream, while star anise offers a hint of something more exotic. This, combined with warm mangoes provides a wickedly delicious pudding.

mango cheeks
with spiced palm sugar ice cream

3 large mangoes

icing sugar, for dusting

Spiced palm sugar ice cream

450 ml milk

300 ml double cream

75 g palm sugar, grated, or soft brown sugar

4 whole star anise

5 egg yolks

Serves 4

To make the ice cream, mix the milk, cream, sugar and star anise into a heavy-based saucepan and heat gently until the mixture just reaches boiling point. Set aside to infuse for 20 minutes. Put the egg yolks into a bowl and beat until pale, then stir in the infused milk. Return to the saucepan and heat gently, stirring constantly, until the mixture is thickened and coats the back of a spoon. Leave to cool completely, then strain.

Put the mixture into an ice-cream maker and freeze according to the manufacturer's instructions. Alternatively, pour into a freezerproof container and freeze for 1 hour until just frozen. Beat vigorously to break up

the ice crystals and return to the freezer. Repeat several times until frozen. Soften in the refrigerator for 20 minutes before serving.

Preheat the barbecue.

Using a sharp knife, cut the cheeks off each mango and put onto a plate. Dust the cut side of each mango cheek with a little icing sugar. Barbecue the cheeks for 2 minutes on each side. Cut the cheeks in half lengthways and serve 3 wedges per person with the ice cream.

meringues
with rosewater cream

Served with rosewater-flavoured cream, these crispy, sugary meringues are truly sublime.

2 large egg whites

115 g caster sugar

200 ml double cream, to serve

1¹/₂ tablespoons rosewater, to serve

a small handful of clean, fresh rose petals, to decorate (optional)

2 baking trays, lined with parchment paper

Makes 8

Preheat the oven to 130°C (250°F) Gas ½.

Put the egg whites in a clean, grease-free bowl and whisk until they form stiff peaks. Whisk in the sugar, one tablespoonful at a time, until the mixture is thick and glossy.

Using two dessert spoons, shape about 16 meringues and place them on the baking trays. Bake for about 2 hours, until crisp and dry. Leave to cool on the trays, then carefully peel away the parchment paper.

To serve, whip the cream until it stands in soft peaks, then fold in the rosewater. Sandwich the meringues together with the cream and arrange on a serving plate. Scatter the rose petals, if using, over the meringues to decorate.

seasonal fruit tarts

Once the rich but simple pastry has been made, these delicious tarts are very easy. You just fill them with seasonal fruit and bake slowly. Choose from apricots, plums, apples, peaches and nectarines. Don't worry if the pastry breaks as you line the tins – just patch any holes or cracks with the trimmings. It will be topped with lovely fruit, so no one will ever know!

600 g plain flour, plus extra for dusting

600 g unsalted butter, cut into cubes and softened

180 g icing sugar, plus extra for dusting

3 egg yolks

1.5 kg fruit, stoned if necessary

500 ml single cream, to serve

2 loose-bottomed flan tins, 28 cm in diameter

Serves 8

To make the pastry, put the flour, butter and icing sugar into a food processor and blend briefly. Add the egg yolks and blend until the mixture forms a ball. Divide in half, wrap both pieces in clingfilm and chill for 40 minutes.

Put one piece of pastry onto a cool, lightly floured surface and gently knead to a flat disc. Roll out into a circle large enough to fit the flan tin, dusting lightly with flour to stop the pastry sticking to the surface. Roll the pastry around a floured rolling pin and unroll over the flan tin. Gently press the pastry into the tin, pressing out any air pockets, then roll the pin over the top of the tin to remove any excess pastry. Repeat with the remaining pastry and flan tin, cover and chill for 25 minutes.

Preheat the oven 180°C (350°F) Gas 4.

Prepare the fruit and slice, halve or leave whole, depending on size, and arrange in the chilled pastry cases. Working from the outside in, cram in all the fruit (it will shrink while cooking). Cook in the preheated oven for 35 minutes, then lower the heat to 150°C (300°F) Gas 2 and cook for a further 55 minutes until the pastry is golden and crisp. Remove and dust generously with icing sugar. Serve hot, warm or cold with cream.

When freshly picked and at the height of their summery sweetness, strawberries are a joy, and they should be eaten simply on their own. At other times, they may need a little assistance to coax out their full potential. The interesting mix of flavours is an echo of the medieval, and often medicinal, use of spices and balsams.

sugared strawberries

To make the spiced sugar, put the cinnamon, peppercorns, sugar and zest in a small spice grinder. Grind in continuous bursts to make a powdery spiced mixture.

Put the strawberries in a bowl, spoon half the mixture on top, gently stirring and mixing to encourage the juices to run. Leave for 10 minutes. Meanwhile, press the ricotta through a sieve into a bowl with the back of a spoon. Mix in the Amaretto liqueur, the remaining spiced sugar and the vinegar to form a cream.

To serve, put spoonfuls of the creamy mixture in small, stemmed glasses or glass or china dishes, then pile the berries on top and sprinkle them with a few extra drops of liqueur.

400 g ripe, red strawberries, washed, dried, hulled and halved

250 g fresh ricotta cheese

1 tablespoon Amaretto liqueur, plus extra to serve

1/2 teaspoon balsamic vinegar

Spiced sugar

1/2 stick of cinnamon, crushed

6 peppercorns, crushed

6 tablespoons caster sugar

8 cm strip of unwaxed lemon zest

Serves 4

traditional english apple tart

Of all the fancy puddings there are, there is nothing to beat a simple baked apple tart. It's quick and simple to make, delicious and it lends itself perfectly to the picnic basket, hot or cold. Slivers of cheddar cheese go well with it too. Children love small apple pies, which can be made in jam tart tins, but you need to stew the apple to a mush and leave it to cool before using.

Preheat the oven to 220°C (425°F) Gas 7.

Put the flour, salt and butter in a large mixing bowl and rub in the butter with your fingertips until the mixture resembles fine breadcrumbs. Add the water and work the mixture together to form a dough. This should be done quickly and lightly with your fingertips or the blade of a round-bladed knife. Alternatively, put the ingredients in a food processor and process until the ingredients are reduced to a dough.

Divide the dough in half and work each half into a neat ball. Sprinkle a clean work surface and a rolling pin with plenty of flour. Set 1 of the pastry balls in the centre of the flour, flatten it with the palm of your hand and shape into a neat circle. Roll the pastry one way, then give it a quarter turn and roll it the other way, shaping the dough back into a circle from time to time. Continue until the pastry is slightly larger than the pie dish.

Roll the pastry around the rolling pin and transfer it carefully to the pie dish, open it out and smooth it to line the dish and the border. Fill with the apple slices, then brush the border with water. Roll out the second ball of dough as before and put this on top of the apples. Trim off the excess pastry with a sharp knife. Press down the border with your thumb to seal it, creating a regular pattern around the edge as you do so. Brush the top of the pie with water and sprinkle with caster sugar.

Set the pie on a baking tray in the centre of the preheated oven and bake for 20 minutes, then lower the heat to 150°C (300°F) Gas 2 and bake for 20 minutes more. Check to see if the fruit is cooked by gently pushing a skewer into it. If it offers resistance, it is not cooked, so cook for a further 10 minutes. If you are going on a picnic immediately, allow to cool a little, wrap in a clean tea towel and a small blanket, and don't forget a pastry slice. Serve warm or cold with sugar and cream.

300 g plain flour

a pinch of sea salt

150 g chilled butter, diced

5 tablespoons chilled water

1 kg cooking apples, peeled, cored and thinly sliced

100 g caster sugar, plus extra to decorate and to serve

cream or natural yoghurt, to serve

a shallow pie dish, 26 cm in diameter, greased

Serves 6

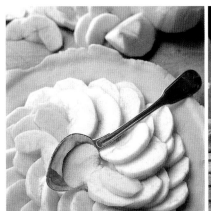

barbecued pears
with spiced honey, walnuts and blue cheese

A simple but delicious end to an outdoor meal – the pears, blue cheese and walnuts perfectly complement one another. Serve on toast with a glass or two of dessert wine. For the best results, choose ripe but firm pears.

50 g shelled walnut pieces

2 tablespoons clear honey

1/4 teaspoon ground cardamom

4 ripe but firm pears

2 tablespoons caster sugar, for dusting

125 g Gorgonzola cheese

slices of toast, to serve

dessert wine, to serve

Serves 4

Put the walnuts into a frying pan, add the honey and cardamom and cook over high heat until the honey bubbles furiously and starts to darken. Immediately pour the mixture onto a sheet of greaseproof paper and leave to cool.

Peel the nuts from the paper and set aside.

Preheat the barbecue. Using a sharp knife, cut the pears into quarters and remove and discard the cores. Cut the pear quarters into thick wedges. Dust lightly with caster sugar and cook over medium-hot coals for about 1½ minutes on each side.

Pile the pears onto slices of toast, sprinkle with the walnuts and serve with some Gorgonzola cheese and a glass of dessert wine.

strawberry and mascarpone trifle

This extraordinarily versatile pudding is perfect for a warm, lazy day. Red fruit always looks magnificent but you could also use blueberries, mangoes and passionfruit. Only about half of the sponge is necessary for this trifle, so freeze the rest for an extra-speedy version next time round. The sponge has a dense, chewy texture to absorb the mint syrup. The mint is a perfect partner for the strawberries, but you could also use fruit juice or sweet wine.

Sponge cake

225 g unsalted butter, softened

225 g caster sugar

4 large eggs, lightly beaten

50 g plain flour

275 g ground almonds

Mint syrup

30 g caster sugar

12 fresh mint leaves, finely chopped

Trifle filling

about 500 g mascarpone cheese

25 g caster sugar

3 egg yolks

250 g raspberries

250 g strawberries

a small handful of fresh mint leaves

a cake tin, 20 cm in diameter, lined with greaseproof paper

Serves 6

Preheat the oven to 180°C (350°F) Gas 4.

To make the sponge cake, put the butter and sugar in a medium bowl and beat with an electric beater until the mixture is pale and creamy. Slowly add the eggs, beating well between each addition. Using a metal spoon, fold in the flour and ground almonds. Spoon into the prepared cake tin and bake in the centre of the preheated oven for 40 minutes until springy to the touch or until a skewer can be removed cleanly when inserted into the middle.

To make the mint syrup, put the sugar, mint and 75 ml water in a small saucepan. Bring to the boil and continue to boil until reduced by one-third.

To make the filling, put the mascarpone, sugar and egg yolks in a bowl. Using an electric beater, beat the mixture until creamy. Using a fork, lightly mash the raspberries to a purée. Chop half the strawberries into small pieces, and cut the remainder in half, leaving the stalks intact for decoration.

To assemble the trifle, break the cake into large pieces and put into a large dish or 6 individual dishes. Moisten the cake with the mint syrup and add some of the mint leaves. Spoon in the raspberry purée, then the chopped strawberries, then the mascarpone. Top with the strawberry halves, then chill in the refrigerator for at least 1 hour before serving.

Frangipane tart is one of those classic recipes that turns a seasonal summer fruit into a luxurious treat. The combination of crisp short pastry, fluffy almond sponge cake and tart summer fruits is a delight. Although it is not difficult to make, it does need time devoted to it, but the end result is well worth the effort.

blueberry frangipane tart

To make the pastry, put the ingredients in a bowl and work them quickly and lightly into a smooth ball with your hands. Wrap in clingfilm and chill in the refrigerator for 1 hour.

Preheat the oven to 180°C (350°F) Gas 4.

To make the frangipane, put the sugar and butter in a bowl and beat until light and creamy. Add the eggs a little at a time, beating well as you do so. Add the cornflour, baking powder and almonds, then gently fold into the mixture.

Sprinkle a clean work surface and rolling pin with plenty of flour. Set the pastry in the centre of the flour, then flatten it with the palm of your hand and shape it into a neat circle. Take the rolling pin and roll the pastry one way, then give it a quarter turn and roll it the other way, shaping the dough back into a circle with your hands from time to time. Continue until the pastry is slighty larger than the tin. Roll the pastry loosely around the rolling pin and transfer it carefully to the greased tin, pressing the pastry carefully into the sides. Trim any overlapping pastry and prick the base with a fork.

Add the blueberries, sprinkle with the sugar, then spoon the frangipane over the top, taking care to seal the fruit completely underneath.

Bake in the preheated oven for 45 minutes or until the frangipane is well risen, golden and springy to the touch. After 25 minutes, open the oven door carefully so as not to allow too much heat to escape and, if the tart is getting too brown, lower the heat to 160°C (325°F) Gas 3 for the final 20 minutes. Serve hot or cold dusted with icing sugar.

150 g blueberries, plums or rhubarb

25 g sugar

icing sugar, to serve

Pastry

100 g plain flour

10 g cornflour

30 g icing sugar

a pinch of salt

60 g unsalted butter, softened

1 small egg yolk

1 tablespoon dry vermouth or iced water

Frangipane

100 g caster sugar

100 g unsalted butter, softened

2 eggs, lightly beaten

2 tablespoons cornflour

2 teaspoons baking powder

100 g ground almonds

a loose-bottomed tart tin or a pie dish, 20–22 cm in diameter, greased

Serves 6

coconut and passionfruit shortbread bake

Dishes that are made the day before are a real bonus, especially for a picnic. With this recipe, not only is there less to do on the day but the shortbread actually improves from resting in a cool cupboard. The sweetness of the coconut is balanced by the tartness of the passionfruit, creating an elegant pudding.

Preheat the oven to 180°C (350°F) Gas 4.

To make the pastry, put the butter and sugar into a bowl and beat with an electric whisk or wooden spoon until creamy. Add the flour and rub it in with your fingertips until the mixture looks like breadcrumbs. Transfer to the prepared cake tin and flatten gently with the palm of your hand and fingers, lining the base and sides of the tin. Chill while you make the filling.

Using a teaspoon, scoop the passionfruit pulp into a small bowl. Put the eggs and sugar into a large bowl and beat with an electric beater until creamy and doubled in volume. Add the desiccated coconut, flour, coconut milk and passionfruit. Using a large metal spoon, fold until evenly mixed.

Spoon the mixture into the chilled pastry case and bake in the preheated oven for 40 minutes. Remove and leave to cool for 10 minutes, then remove from the tin to a serving plate. Dust with icing sugar and serve with a mixture of Greek yoghurt and cream, or with ice cream.

100 g unsalted butter

100 g caster sugar

150 g plain flour

Filling

7 passionfruit, halved

3 eggs

75 g caster sugar

75 g desiccated coconut

60 g plain flour

150 ml coconut milk

1 tablespoon icing sugar, for dusting

Greek yoghurt and cream, or vanilla ice cream, to serve

a springform cake tin, 20 cm in diameter, lightly greased

Serves 8

This barbecued sweet works well with stone fruits too, such as plums, peaches or nectarines.

grilled figs
with almond mascarpone cream

150 g mascarpone cheese

1/2 teaspoon vanilla extract

1 tablespoon toasted ground almonds

1 tablespoon Marsala wine

1 tablespoon clear honey

1 tablespoon caster sugar

1 teaspoon ground cardamom

8–10 figs, halved

Serves 4

Put the mascarpone cheese, vanilla extract, almonds, Marsala wine and honey into a bowl and beat well. Set aside in the refrigerator until required.

Put the sugar and ground cardamom into a separate bowl and mix well, then carefully dip the cut surface of the figs into the mixture.

Preheat the barbecue, then cook the figs over medium-hot coals for 1–2 minutes on each side until charred and softened.

Transfer the grilled figs to 4 serving bowls and serve with the almond mascarpone cream.

An apricot tart, glazed and warm from the oven, is as welcome as the sun bursting through the clouds. This version, needing no flan tins or split-second timing, is an effortless dessert after a carefree day spent outdoors.

apricot tart

375 g ready-rolled puff pastry, chilled

1 egg, beaten, for glazing

500 g ripe apricots, halved and stoned, the stones reserved

100 g apricot jam

1 tablespoon freshly squeezed lemon juice

4 tablespoons vanilla sugar (page 145)

sifted icing sugar, to decorate (optional)

Serves 4–6

Preheat the oven to 220°C (425°F) Gas 7.

Unroll the pastry and cut out a circle 25 cm in diameter. Re-roll the offcuts and make 4 strips about 2 x 25 cm. Set aside.

Transfer the pastry to a lightly oiled baking tray. Leaving a 2-cm border all round, prick the rest of the pastry with a fork.

Brush the unpricked border of the pastry with the beaten egg. Place the pastry strips on it, cutting the ends to be joined on the diagonal and pressing them neatly together. These will puff up when baked, and act like a wall around the fruit. Brush beaten egg all over the pastry, including the pricked area. Bake blind for 20 minutes, or until golden and risen at the edges. Prick once again.

Meanwhile, crack open 6 of the apricot stones. Remove and shred the kernels.

Cut each apricot half into 6 segments. Arrange them, flesh upwards, on the pastry. Scatter the shredded kernels over the top.

Put the jam and lemon juice in a small bowl and stir until smooth. Using a pastry brush, paint this glaze all over the fruit. Sprinkle on the vanilla sugar, then bake for 20 minutes, until the apricots are soft, fragrant and slightly browned at the tips. Serve warm, dusted with icing sugar, if liked.

Variation Red plums, nectarines or peaches can be used in place of apricots, but do not use the kernels of plums.

lime mousse with lemon sauce

Make this mousse the night before, as there is nothing worse than willing an unset mousse to set before serving.

1 sachet powdered gelatine

3 eggs, separated

75 g caster sugar

grated zest and freshly squeezed juice of 3 unwaxed limes

150 ml double cream

Lemon sauce

4 tablespoons caster sugar

finely grated zest and freshly squeezed juice of 2 unwaxed lemons

Serves 8

Put 3 tablespoons hot water into a small bowl and sprinkle in the gelatine. Put the bowl into a warm oven or over a pan of simmering water, about 10 minutes. When completely dissolved, remove to room temperature and leave to cool a little.

Put the egg yolks and sugar into a large bowl and beat with electric beaters until frothy and creamy. Add the lime zest and juice and beat well. Add the dissolved gelatine and beat again, then set aside for 5 minutes. Whisk the cream until soft peaks form, then fold into the lime mixture. Wash the beaters well and whisk the egg whites until stiff. Add to the lime mixture and whisk briefly. Spoon into individual pots or one serving bowl. Chill for at least 2 hours, or overnight.

To make the sauce, put the sugar, lemon juice and half the zest into a small saucepan and mix. Bring to the boil, then simmer for 1 minute. Remove from the heat and cool completely to a syrupy sauce. If it is a little too thick, stir in a small amount of water. Sprinkle the remaining lemon zest over the mousse and serve with the sauce.

lavender shortbread

Homemade shortbread is unbelievably easy to make. Cornflour will make it smoother; ground rice or fine semolina more crumbly and rustic.

75 g caster sugar, plus extra for sprinkling

175 g unsalted butter, softened

1/4–1/2 teaspoon concentrated lavender essence or 1 tablespoon finely chopped dried lavender flowers

175 g plain flour

75 g cornflour, ground rice or fine semolina

a shallow 27 x 18 cm baking tin

Makes 18 shortbreads

Preheat the oven to 150°F (300°C) Gas 2.

Put the sugar and butter in a food processor and process until light and fluffy (or beat together with an electric hand-held whisk). Add the lavender essence or flowers and whizz again. Add half the flour and pulse to incorporate, then add the remaining flour and pulse again. Add the cornflour

and pulse again until incorporated. (Alternatively, add in stages, by hand, beating with a wooden spoon then bring the mixture together with your hands.) Tip the mixture into a baking tin and spread out until even. Mark the shortbread with a sharp knife, dividing it into 18 squares, and prick lightly with the prongs of a fork.

Bake in the preheated oven for about 40–45 minutes until pale gold in colour. Sprinkle with the remaining sugar, put back in the oven and cook for another 5 minutes. Remove the tin from the oven, set aside for 10 minutes, then cut along the lines you've marked again. Remove the shortbread squares carefully with a palate knife and lay on a wire rack to finish cooling. Store in an airtight tin.

sparkling shiraz and summer berry jellies

9 sheets of gelatine (or enough to set 750 ml of liquid)

750 ml sparkling Shiraz or other sparkling red wine

600 g mixed fresh red berries, such as strawberries, raspberries, blackberries, blueberries, blackcurrants or redcurrants

2–3 tablespoons caster sugar, depending on how ripe your berries are

6–8 tablespoons homemade sugar syrup* or shop-bought gomme

8 glasses or small glass serving dishes

Serves 8

Put the gelatine in a flat dish and sprinkle over 4 tablespoons cold water. Leave to soak for 3 minutes until soft. Heat the wine in a microwave or saucepan until hot but not boiling. Tip the gelatine into the wine and stir to dissolve, then set aside to cool. Rinse the berries, cut the strawberries into halves or quarters, then put them in a shallow bowl, sprinkle over the sugar and leave to macerate. Check the liquid jelly for sweetness, adding sugar syrup to taste.

Put an assortment of berries in the glasses, then pour over enough jelly to cover them. Put in the refrigerator to chill. As soon as the jelly has set (about 1 hour) add the rest of the fruit and jelly. Return the jellies to the refrigerator to set for another ¾–1 hour before serving.

* To make the sugar syrup, dissolve 125 g sugar in 150 ml water. Heat gently together in a pan. When all the grains are dissolved, bring to the boil and simmer for 2–3 minutes. Use immediately or cool and store for up to 2 weeks in the refrigerator.

sparkling nectarine and blueberry jellies

9 sheets of gelatine (or enough to set 750 ml of liquid)

750 ml sparkling peach-flavoured wine

3 ripe nectarines

2 tablespoons freshly squeezed lemon juice

200 g blueberries

8 glasses or small glass serving dishes

Serves 8–10

Put the gelatine in a flat dish and sprinkle over 4 tablespoons cold water. Leave to soak for 3 minutes until soft. Heat the wine in a microwave or saucepan until hot but not boiling. Tip the gelatine into the wine and stir to dissolve, then set aside to cool. Cut the nectarines into cubes and sprinkle with the lemon juice. Put a few blueberries and cubes of nectarine in the bottom of each glass then pour over jelly to cover. Put in the refrigerator to chill. As soon as the jelly has set, add the remaining fruit and jelly. Return to the refrigerator to set for another ¾–1 hour before serving.

120 ml medium-dry or sweet Champagne, or sparkling white wine

6 gelatine leaves or 1 1/2 sachets (11 g) gelatine granules

760 ml yellow Chartreuse liqueur

100 ml Muscat de Beaumes-de-Venise

50 g wild or small cultivated strawberries, quartered

100 g raspberries

75 g redcurrants, half left on the sprigs to decorate, or 8 fresh cherries, plus 8 to decorate

4 goblets

Serves 4

scented fruit jelly

Tall goblets of sweet, refreshingly cool, scented wine jelly, studded with pretty little summer fruits... what could be more perfect? Aim to make this dessert when wild strawberries or fraises de garrigue are available: their extraordinary intensity helps to make this recipe a remarkable one.

Put 100 ml of the Champagne in a heatproof measuring jug, add the gelatine and leave to soften and swell for 10 minutes. Mix the remaining Champagne with the Chartreuse and Muscat.

Heat the gelatine mixture over boiling water, or in a microwave on high in 20-second bursts, until the gelatine is completely dissolved. Pour in the Chartreuse mixture, stir, then cool over iced water. During the following steps, set the gelatine over the pan of boiling water now and again to keep it barely liquid.

Put a quarter of the strawberries into each goblet. Pour in a quarter of the gelatine mixture, then refrigerate until firm.

Repeat this layering process with each type of fruit, letting each layer set before adding the next. Place any remaining gelatine mixture over the iced water to set firmly, then chop it into tiny pieces.

Pile some of the chopped gelatine onto each dessert and decorate with the reserved sprigs of redcurrants or the cherries. Serve cool or chilled.

pomegranate granita

This once hard-to-find fruit, a native of the Middle East, has a thick waxy skin enclosing hundreds of jewel-like ruby seeds. The juice is hailed as a great antioxidant and is now widely available in many shops.

200 g caster sugar

600 ml pomegranate juice

pomegranate seeds, to decorate (optional)

Makes about 600 ml, serves 4–6

In a large shallow plastic container, stir the sugar into the juice until dissolved.

Cover and freeze for 2 hours or until the mixture starts to look mushy.

Using a fork, break up the ice crystals and finely mash them. Return the granita to the freezer for another 2 hours, mashing every 30 minutes, until the ice forms fine, even crystals. After the final mashing return to the freezer for at least an hour before serving. Decorate with the fresh pomegranate seeds, if using.

orange and lemon granita

Zing zing zing! Your taste buds won't know what's hit them. Zesty doesn't even begin to describe this wide-awake, citrus assault on the senses.

115 g caster sugar

6 oranges

2 unwaxed lemons

Makes about 600 ml, serves 4–6

Put the sugar and 200 ml water into a saucepan. Pare thin strips of zest from 1 orange and 1 lemon and add them to the sugar and water. Heat gently, stirring until the sugar has completely dissolved. Bring to the boil and then remove from the heat and leave to cool. When cold, strain the liquid into a large shallow plastic container.

Juice the fruit and stir into the syrup to combine. Freeze for 2 hours. With a fork, mash up any crystals that have formed. Return to the freezer for another 2 hours and repeat the mashing process. Freeze again for at least 1 more hour before serving.

This would be the perfect ending to an Eastern-inspired meal. Star anise and mandarin oranges are natural partners, as both originate in China. The star anise not only adds a wonderful liquorice flavour, it also looks stunning and makes for a very stylish decoration.

star anise and mandarin orange granita

150 g sugar

6 whole star anise

20 mandarin oranges

Makes about 600 ml, serves 4–6

Put the sugar and 200 ml water in a saucepan and heat gently, stirring until the sugar has completely dissolved. Add the star anise and simmer without stirring for 2 minutes. Remove from the heat and leave to cool.

Cut a slice off the top and bottom of each mandarin, then slice away the peel and pith. Chop the flesh roughly and process in a food processor until almost smooth. Press the resulting pulp through a sieve into a large shallow plastic container. Strain the syrup into the same container, reserving the star anise. Mix well, cover and freeze for 2 hours or until the mixture starts to look mushy.

Using a fork, break up and finely mash the ice crystals. Return the granita to the freezer for another 2 hours, mashing every 30 minutes, until the ice forms fine, even crystals. After the final mashing return to the freezer for at least an hour before serving. Decorate with the reserved star anise, if you wish.

toasted coconut ice cream
with grilled pineapple

Toasting the desiccated coconut enriches the ice cream and gives it a lovely nutty flavour.

1 pineapple, medium or small, with leafy top if possible

100 g soft brown sugar

100 g unsalted butter

100 ml dark rum

Ice cream

25 g desiccated coconut

450 ml double cream

300 ml coconut milk

100 g caster sugar

5 egg yolks

Serves 6

To make the ice cream, put the coconut into a dry frying pan and toast, stirring over medium heat for 2–3 minutes until evenly browned. Transfer to a saucepan, then add the cream, coconut milk and sugar. Heat gently until it just reaches boiling point.

Put the egg yolks into a bowl and beat with a wooden spoon until pale. Stir in about 2 tablespoons of the hot coconut mixture, then return the mixture to the pan. Heat gently, stirring constantly until the mixture thickens enough to coat the back of the wooden spoon. Remove the pan from the heat and leave to cool completely.

When cold, strain the mixture and freeze in an ice-cream maker according to the manufacturer's instructions. Transfer to the freezer until required. Alternatively, pour the cold mixture into a plastic container and freeze for 5 hours, beating at hourly intervals with a balloon whisk.

Preheat the barbecue.

To prepare the pineapple, cut it lengthways into wedges (including the leafy top) and remove the core sections.

Put the sugar, butter and rum into a small saucepan and heat until the sugar dissolves. Brush a little of the mixture over the pineapple wedges, then cook them on the preheated barbecue or on a ridged

stove-top grill pan for 2 minutes on each side until charred and tender. Remove from the heat and, holding the flesh with a fork, cut between the skin and flesh with a sharp knife. Cut the flesh into segments to make it easier to eat, then reassemble the wedges. Serve with the ice cream and remaining rum sauce, about 2 tablespoons each.

kiwi and stem ginger sorbet

This wonderfully speckled, pale green sorbet is made using ripe kiwis and is given a lively aromatic flavour by the addition of stem ginger. For a stronger flavour, omit the stem ginger and use a teaspoon of freshly peeled and grated ginger instead.

115 g golden caster sugar

8 ripe kiwi fruit, peeled and roughly chopped

1 egg white, lightly beaten

2 tablespoons stem ginger, drained and finely chopped

an ice-cream maker (optional)

Makes 600 ml, serves 4–6

Place the sugar and 300 ml water in a small saucepan and heat gently until the sugar has dissolved. Bring to the boil and remove from the heat. Allow to cool and then chill.

Place the kiwi fruit in a blender and process until smooth. Add this to the chilled syrup and stir to mix well.

If using an ice-cream maker, churn the mixture until thick, add the egg white and stem ginger and churn until firm enough to scoop. Freeze until ready to serve.

If making the sorbet by hand, pour the mixture into a shallow freezer-proof container, stir in the egg white and allow to freeze for 3–4 hours. Place in a food processor, process until smooth and return to the freezer, repeating this process once more. Stir in the stem ginger and freeze for 3–4 hours until firm.

You can experiment with different flavours with this delightfully elegant herby sorbet. Try Earl Grey tea with lemon balm, or jasmine tea with lemon and ginger. The wafers go well with all kinds of ice creams and sorbets.

lemon, thyme and green tea sorbet
with pistachio and lemon wafers

3 green tea teabags

200 g sugar

1 tablespoon fresh thyme sprigs, preferably lemon thyme

finely grated zest of 2 unwaxed lemons

freshly squeezed juice of up to 1½ lemons

1 egg white, lightly beaten (optional)

Pistachio and lemon wafers

125 g unsalted butter, softened

125 g vanilla sugar*

grated zest of 1 unwaxed lemon

1 egg, beaten

200 g plain flour

2 tablespoons potato flour or cornflour

a pinch of sea salt

100 g shelled, unsalted pistachio nuts, blanched and chopped

an ice-cream maker (optional)

2 heavy baking trays, greased

Serves 6–8

Place the teabags in a bowl and pour over 500 ml cold water, cover and leave overnight. The next day, dissolve the sugar in 250 ml water in a saucepan over low heat and bring to the boil. Take off the heat and pour into a heatproof bowl, then add the thyme and lemon zest. Leave the syrup to cool, cover, then chill in the refrigerator overnight.

The next day, strain both mixtures into a bowl or jug and stir in lemon juice to taste. Chill, then churn in an ice-cream maker according to the manufacturer's instructions, and then freeze. If making by hand, turn into a freezerproof container to make a shallow layer and freeze until hard around the edges. Turn into a food processor, add the egg white and process until smooth. Repeat the freezing and beating once more, then allow to freeze firm.

To make the wafers, cream the butter and sugar until light. Beat in the lemon zest, then the egg. Sift in the flours and salt, then stir in the pistachios. Form the dough into a roll shape, approximately 5 cm in diameter, then put it in the centre of a sheet of greaseproof paper. Roll up the paper to enclose the roll of dough, then chill until firm, at least 3 hours or overnight.

Preheat the oven to 180°C (350°F) Gas 4.

Using a sharp knife, cut off thin slices from the dough, 4–5 mm thick, and lay on the baking trays. Bake in the preheated oven for 12–15 minutes until browned around the edges. Leave to cool on a wire rack.

Leave the sorbet to soften in the refrigerator for 15–20 minutes, then serve with a few wafers for each person. Store the remaining wafers in an airtight tin.

* To make the vanilla sugar, bury 2 or 3 vanilla pods in a jar of caster sugar and leave for 1 week, after which the sugar will take on the aroma of vanilla. Or, for a quick version, grind 3 tablespoons caster sugar with a small piece of vanilla pod in a clean coffee grinder.

lemon yoghurt ice cream

A light, zingy yoghurt-based ice cream is lovely to serve with ripe summer berries. Make sure you choose a good-quality, creamy, full-fat yoghurt or the ice cream will be far too acidic and the texture too icy.

500 ml natural yoghurt

grated zest and freshly squeezed juice of 2 unwaxed lemons

100 g caster sugar

an ice-cream maker

Serves 4–6

Put the yoghurt, lemon zest and juice and sugar in a bowl and stir until smooth. Churn in an ice-cream maker, then transfer to a freezer-proof container and freeze until ready to serve.

Use good, creamy, plain yoghurt for this recipe and you will be rewarded with a delectable ice cream. Frozen fruit works well in this recipe too, just defrost them first. They will ooze juice, so there is no need to warm them through. The colour of this ice cream is so redolent of summer that you'll be tempted to make it in the dark winter months just to transport yourself to sunnier times.

summer berry yoghurt ice cream

500 g mixed summer berries, such as strawberries, blackberries and raspberries

150 g caster sugar

500 g natural yoghurt

an ice-cream maker

Serves 4

Warm the berries and sugar in a saucepan over low heat for several minutes, until the fruit begins to release its juices. Transfer to a food processor and blend to a purée. Push the purée through a fine-meshed nylon sieve to remove the seeds. Stir in the yoghurt.

Churn in an ice-cream maker until frozen. Transfer to a freezer-proof container and freeze until ready to serve.

drinks

ginger lemonade

There is something rather satisfying about being served a good homemade lemonade, particularly when you're on a summer picnic.

10 cm fresh ginger, peeled and very thinly sliced

freshly squeezed juice of 4 lemons

1 lemon, sliced

75 g sugar

crushed ice

Serves 4

Put the ginger, lemon juice, sliced lemon and sugar in a heatproof jug and pour on 1 litre boiling water. Mix well and leave to steep for 2 hours. Chill, then serve poured over crushed ice.

Variation If you don't like lemons, use limes or oranges and, for a really clean taste, add fresh mint. For something stronger, add a shot of vodka to each glass.

2–3 cooking apples, unpeeled, chopped into small pieces

sugar, to taste

freshly squeezed juice of 1 lemon

sparkling water, to serve

Serves 4

apple lemonade

This recipe is best made with cooking apples – they turn to delicious foam when boiled. For a quicker result, use fresh apple juice, omit the sugar, add the lemon juice and fill with sparkling water.

Put the apples in a saucepan, cover with cold water, bring to the boil and simmer until soft. Strain, pressing the pulp through the strainer with a spoon. Add sugar to taste, stir until dissolved, then leave to cool.

To serve, pack a jug with ice, half-fill the glass with the apple juice, add the lemon juice and top with sparkling water.

homemade lemonade

You will need a juicer to make this delicious lemonade – it's almost worth buying one just to make it.

150 g caster sugar

4 large juicy unwaxed lemons, plus 1 extra, sliced, to garnish

1 litre still or sparkling mineral water, chilled

a few sprigs of fresh mint

a juicer

Serves 6–8

Put the sugar in a saucepan with 150 ml water. Heat over low heat, stirring until the sugar has completely dissolved, then bring to the boil and boil for 5 minutes without stirring. Take off the heat and leave to cool. Cut 2 of the lemons into small chunks and pass through the feeder tube of a juicer. They should produce about 150 ml thick juice. Squeeze the remaining lemons (again, that should yield about 150 ml) and add to the other juice. Stir in the sugar syrup you have made.

Chill the lemon concentrate until ready to use. Either pour into a large jugful of ice and pour in an equal amount of chilled still or sparkling mineral water or pour a couple of shots of lemonade into a tumbler full of ice and top up with chilled mineral water. Garnish with lemon slices and sprigs of mint.

Variation To make raspberry lemonade, purée (in a food processor or force through a nylon sieve) 150 g of fresh or frozen raspberries and sweeten with 2 tablespoons sugar syrup (see above). Stir into the lemonade base and dilute as described. Decorate with lemon slices and a few whole raspberries.

When making iced tea, it's best to add the tea bags to cold water rather than boiling water to avoid the unpleasant scum that can appear on the surface.

iced ginger tea

50 g fresh ginger, peeled and finely sliced

4 tea bags

2 limes, sliced

lemonade

Serves 6

Put the sliced ginger into a large jug, pour over 1 litre boiling water and leave until cold. Add the tea bags and chill for 1 hour.

Strain the tea into a clean jug, add the slices of lime and ice cubes, then top up with lemonade.

Iced lemon coffee can be just as refreshing as iced lemon tea on a hot day. It may sound a little strange, but it's very thirst-quenching.

iced lemon coffee

500 ml freshly brewed espresso coffee

caster sugar, to taste

1 tablespoon freshly squeezed lemon juice

lemon peel, to serve

Serves 6

Pour the coffee into a large jug, add sugar to taste and stir until dissolved. Leave to cool, then chill until very cold.

Half-fill glasses with ice cubes. Add the lemon juice to the coffee, then pour into the glasses and serve with a twist of lemon peel.

Always make fresh juices just before serving, because they can discolour and separate quickly.

strawberry, pear and orange frappé

400 g strawberries, hulled

4 pears, quartered and cored

300 ml freshly squeezed orange juice

a juicer

Serves 4

Push the strawberries and pears through a juicer and transfer to a jug. Add the orange juice and pour into glasses half filled with ice cubes. Serve at once.

A lovely refreshing cordial with a delicious kick of ginger – perfect for a picnic.

ginger and lime cordial

150 g fresh ginger

2 unwaxed limes, sliced

500 g granulated sugar

unwaxed lime wedges, to serve

sparkling water, to serve

1 sterilized bottle, 750 ml (page 4)

Makes about 750 ml

Using a sharp knife, peel and thinly slice the ginger, then pound lightly with a rolling pin. Put into a saucepan, add the lime slices and 1 litre water, bring to the boil, part-cover with a lid and simmer gently for 45 minutes. Remove from the heat, add the sugar and stir until dissolved. Leave to cool, strain and pour the cordial into a sterilized bottle. Seal and store until ready to use.

When ready to serve, pour a little cordial into glasses, add ice and lime wedges and top up with sparkling water.

Almond milk is a classic North African and Middle Eastern drink. Served chilled on a hot day, it is both nourishing and refreshing. Traditionally, the 'milk' is extracted from the almonds but modern recipes often add cow's milk. In Morocco, orange flower water or fresh orange rind is added to the drink to give it a floral or zesty lift and, on special occasions, rose petals are floated on the surface of each glass.

almond milk

250 g blanched almonds

125 g caster sugar

600 ml water

1–2 tablespoons orange flower water

rose petals, orange zest or ground cinnamon, to serve

Serves 4

Using a pestle and mortar or an electric blender, pound the almonds with half the sugar to a smooth paste – add a splash of water if the paste gets too stiff.

Put the water and the remaining sugar in a heavy-based saucepan and bring it to the boil, stirring until the sugar has dissolved. Stir in the almond paste and simmer for 5 minutes.

Turn off the heat and stir in the orange flower water. Leave the mixture to cool in the pan to enable the flavours to mingle. Once cool, strain the mixture through a muslin cloth, or a fine, plastic sieve (don't use a metal one because it will taint the flavour and colour of the almonds). Use your hand to squeeze all the milk out of the almonds.

Pour the cloudy liquid into a jug and chill in the refrigerator. When ready to serve, give it a stir and pour the milk into glasses over ice cubes, or place the glasses in the freezer so they are frosty when served. Decorate with rose petals, a fine curl of orange peel or a pinch of ground cinnamon.

chai vanilla milkshake

The flavours of chai are wonderful combined with vanilla ice cream to make an unctuous milkshake.

1 litre whole milk

75 g light muscovado sugar

2 tablespoons black tea leaves

1 vanilla pod, split lengthways

1/4 teaspoon ground cinnamon

8 cardamom pods

1/4 teaspoon ground allspice

3 scoops of vanilla ice cream

ice-cube trays

Serves 4

Put 800 ml of the milk, the sugar, tea leaves, vanilla pod, cinnamon, cardamom and allspice in a saucepan and bring to the boil. Reduce the heat and simmer gently for 5 minutes, then turn off the heat, cover and leave for 10 minutes. Strain into the ice-cube trays and freeze until solid. Freeze 4 tall glasses.

When ready to serve, pop the frozen chai cubes in a blender with the remaining milk and the ice cream and blend until smooth.

moroccan fresh mint tea

Taking a glass of fresh mint tea is an important ritual in North Africa and it is thought rude if you drink any less than two cups. The Chinese green tea used for this popular drink is Gunpowder tea, which is crisp and fresh. The tea is rolled into a small pellet, which most probably accounts for the name.

2 tablespoons Chinese Gunpowder green tea leaves or 3 green tea bags

a handful of fresh mint leaves

75 g granulated sugar

sugar cubes, to serve

2 heatproof glasses

kitchen thermometer (optional)

Serves 2

Put the tea leaves in a warmed teapot with two-thirds of the mint leaves and all the sugar. Heat 600 ml water to 82°C (180°F), just before the water starts to bubble, and pour into the teapot. Leave to steep for 6 minutes. Put the remaining mint in 2 heatproof glasses. Strain the tea into the glasses and serve with sugar cubes, to taste.

jamaican iced ginger sorrel tea

Jamaican sorrel is the flower of a native hibiscus, sold fresh or dried in Caribbean stores or in health food shops, where it is sometimes labelled as 'red hibiscus tea'. In Australia and New Zealand, it's known as 'rosella' and is used to make jam. It has an unusual, sophisticated taste – not unlike cranberry juice – and, if you like vaguely bitter flavours, you'll love it!

3 cm fresh ginger, peeled and sliced or grated

4 tablespoons dried sorrel flowers or hibiscus tea

4 tablespoons sugar

a twist of lime, to serve

Serves 4–8

Put the ginger, sorrel and sugar into a cafetière. Pour over boiling water. When the liquid is a light purple (this happens fast!) push the plunger, then serve immediately, or cool and chill. Serve over ice with a twist of lime. To serve as a longer drink, top up with ginger ale, soda or mineral water.

Variation For sorrel rum cocktail, put 4 tablespoons dried sorrel, a twist of orange peel, 1 cinnamon stick, 6 cloves and 200–400 g sugar, according to taste, into a cafetière. Pour over 1.5 litres boiling water, stir well, then push the plunger. Add 2 extra cloves and a cinnamon stick to the top, cool and chill. To serve, pour over ice, then add a jigger of rum and a cinnamon stick for swizzling.

iced peach and elderflower tea

The tea you use for this recipe should have some bitterness and tannins to contrast against the sweetness of both the elderflower and peach juice.

6 black tea bags, such as Keemun or English Breakfast

1.5 litres just-boiled water

100 ml elderflower cordial

250 ml peach juice

peach slices and raspberries, to serve

Serves 6–8

Put the tea bags in a large heatproof jug or bowl and pour over the hot water. Leave to steep for 3–4 minutes, then remove the tea bags and leave to cool until lukewarm. Add the elderflower cordial and peach juice and give it a good stir. Leave until cold, then add the peach slices, raspberries and ice cubes to serve.

green tea martini

1 tablespoon granulated sugar

100 ml hot green tea

60 ml citron vodka

2 teaspoons Cointreau

an orange twist, to garnish

a cocktail shaker

2 Martini glasses

Serves 2

Put the sugar in the hot green tea and stir until it has dissolved. Leave to cool. Pour into a cocktail shaker with the vodka, Cointreau and some ice cubes. Shake well and strain into 2 Martini glasses. Garnish with an orange twist.

g & tea

2 tablespoons granulated sugar

3 tablespoons hot black tea

3 tablespoons gin

freshly squeezed juice of ^{1}/2 lemon, plus 1 lemon wedge, to serve

200 ml tonic water

a highball glass

Serves 1

Put the sugar in the hot black tea and stir until it has dissolved. Leave to cool. Add the gin and lemon juice and stir. Fill a highball glass with some ice cubes, pour over the tea mixture and top with the tonic water. Garnish with the lemon wedge.

blackberry tea vodka

1 litre vodka

4 blackberry tea bags

300 g granulated sugar

450 g blackberries, plus extra to serve

ice cubes or soda water, to serve

2 sterilized bottles or containers, 750 ml each (page 4)

Makes 1.5 litres

Put 100 ml of the vodka in a bowl and drop in the tea bags. Cover and leave to steep overnight. Divide the tea mixture between the sterilized bottles. Put half the remaining vodka, sugar and blackberries in each bottle. Cover and refrigerate, shaking each day to dissolve the sugar and mix the flavours. After about a month, strain through a fine sieve, discard the berries and rebottle. Serve on ice or with soda water, with extra blackberries.

stick drinks

Stick drinks, also known as caprioskas, are cocktails made by mashing fruits and sugar together with a stick, usually a lollipop stick, or a citrus press. You can use almost any fruit as long as you include chopped limes and sugar.

lime and mint stick drink

12 large fresh mint leaves

2 teaspoons brown sugar

1 lime, finely diced

2 large shots Bacardi rum

soda water

a cocktail shaker or jug

2 cocktail glasses

Serves 2

Put the mint leaves, sugar and lime into a cocktail shaker and mash with a stick or spoon until quite pulpy.

Fill 2 cocktail glasses with ice to chill them thoroughly, then tip the ice into the mashed mint mixture. Add the Bacardi to the mixture, shake well, then pour back into the glasses. Add a little soda water and serve.

kiwifruit, passionfruit and lime sticky

1 large lime, diced

1 large kiwifruit, peeled and diced

12 fresh mint leaves

3 teaspoons caster sugar

1 large passionfruit, halved

2 large shots vodka

a cocktail shaker or jug

2 cocktail glasses

Serves 2

Put the lime and kiwifruit into a cocktail shaker, add the mint, sugar and passionfruit pulp and seeds. Mash well until pulpy.

Fill 2 cocktail glasses with ice to chill them thoroughly, then tip the ice into the kiwifruit mixture. Add the vodka, shake or stir well, then pour back into the glasses.

There are so many cocktails that it is almost impossible to create a new one. This marriage of two classics, Champagne and mimosa cocktails, uses prosecco wine and blood red orange juice. Prosecco is a sparkling wine made in the Veneto and sold by the glass in bars and restaurants all over Venice; hence the name Bloody Venetian.

bloody venetian

2 tablespoons caster sugar

freshly squeezed juice of 1 lemon

750 ml chilled prosecco or sparkling wine

60 ml Cointreau

60 ml brandy

750 ml chilled blood orange juice

12 cocktail glasses

a cocktail shaker or punch bowl

Serves 12

To prepare the cocktail glasses, put the sugar on a plate and spread it out evenly. Wet the rim of a glass with lemon juice and dip it into the sugar, twisting the glass as you do so to get a good covering. Repeat with the other glasses.

When ready to serve, pour the Cointreau, brandy and orange juice into a cocktail shaker and shake well. Alternatively, pour the ingredients into a punch bowl and stir well.

Place a few ice cubes in each of 12 glasses, then pour or ladle the cocktail carefully into the glasses, taking care not to wet the sugar crust. Divide the prosecco between the glasses and serve immediately.

This is a variation of the Cuban classic, the mojito. With the glass packed with crushed ice, this cocktail makes the perfect summer drink. Add a little extra sugar for the sweeter tooth or a little more lime for a citrus twist.

herba buena

50 ml gold tequila

15 ml freshly squeezed lime juice

1 brown rock sugar cube

5 sprigs of fresh mint, plus 1 to garnish

crushed ice

soda water, to top up

a highball glass

Serves 1

Muddle all the ingredients apart from the ice and soda water in a highball glass using a barspoon. Add the ice, muddle again and top up with the soda. Stir gently, garnish with a mint sprig and serve with two straws.

virginia mint julep

This recipe comes from an old American cookbook, *The Williamsburg Art of Cookery or Accomplished Gentlewoman's Companion* of 1742. This is the advice printed with it: 'Two Things will inevitably ruin any Julep, the first of which is too much Sugar, and the second is too little Whiskey'. Heeding the warning, the original quantity of sugar has been reduced here from 6 to 4 tablespoons. The original recipe called for whiskey made from corn, but if you can't source it, your favourite whiskey will do.

5 sprigs of fresh mint

4 tablespoons caster sugar

whiskey distilled from corn, such as Kentucky Straight Corn Whiskey

crushed ice

Serves 4

Divide the leaves from 1 sprig of mint between 4 tall glasses. Add 1 tablespoon of the sugar to each glass and crush together well using a swizzle stick. Add 1 tablespoon of water to each glass to dissolve. Fill the glasses with crushed ice and add as much whiskey as the ice will take. Stir well until the glasses are frosted on the outside, taking care not to wet the outside of the glass. Decorate each glass with the remaining mint sprigs and serve.

This fresh-fruit cooler always appeals due to the nature of the ingredients – there just seems to be something about raspberries in cocktails that everyone enjoys.

raspberry rickey

4 raspberries

50 ml vodka

20 ml freshly squeezed lime juice

1 dash Chambord (raspberry liqueur)

soda water, to top up

a lime wedge, to garnish

a highball glass

Serves 1

Muddle the raspberries in the bottom of a highball glass. Fill with ice, add the remaining ingredients and stir gently. Garnish with a lime wedge and serve with two straws.

diablo

A long refreshing cocktail with a delicate hint of blackcurrant.

50 ml gold tequila

15 ml freshly squeezed lime juice

15 ml crème de cassis

ginger ale

crushed ice

redcurrants, to garnish

a hurricane glass

Serves 1

Build all the ingredients in a hurricane glass filled with crushed ice. Garnish with a small bunch of redcurrants. Serve with two straws.

old-fashioned white wine cup

The great virtue of white wine cups is that you can use a really basic, inexpensive dry white wine as the base. In fact, it's a positive advantage to do so. Most modern whites have too much up-front fruit flavour and alcohol for this delicate, quintessentially English summery drink.

2 bottles very dry white wine, such as basic Vin Blanc or Muscadet, 750 ml each, chilled

750 ml soda water, chilled

100–125 ml sugar syrup (page 140) or shop-bought gomme

50–100 ml brandy

orange, lemon, apple, kiwi, strawberry and cucumber slices, to serve

a few fresh mint or borage leaves, to garnish

Serves 16

Mix the wine and soda in a jug and add sugar syrup and brandy to taste. Prepare the fruit and add to the mix, together with ice cubes, just before serving. Serve in wine glasses, garnished with the mint.

This punch is very strong, so if you want to give people more than one glass, make it gentler by adding some ginger beer or mineral water. If you can't find ginger wine, use dry sherry, then add a chunk of fresh ginger, peeled and finely sliced.

jamaican punch

freshly squeezed juice of 3 limes

1/2 bottle ginger wine, 375 ml

1 bottle white rum or vodka, 750 ml

sugar, to taste

3 limes, sliced

3 lemons, sliced

1 starfruit, sliced (optional)

1 pineapple, cut lengthways into long wedges, then crossways into triangles

a few sprigs of fresh mint, to serve

Serves 16–20

Put the lime juice, ginger wine, rum or vodka and sugar into a jug and stir until the sugar dissolves.

Fill a punch bowl with ice, add the sliced fruit and pour over the ginger wine mixture. Stir well and serve with sprigs of mint.

A pretty spritzer to cool a hot brow during a summer picnic.

white wine spritzer

1 bottle white wine, 750 ml, chilled

1 litre sparkling mineral water, chilled

400 g frozen white grapes

Serves 8

Put the chilled white wine, mineral water and frozen grapes in a large jug and mix well. Serve in your favourite large glasses.

Cook's tip Frozen fruit cubes are great taken on picnics to chill drinks. They do not melt as quickly as ordinary ice cubes and children love eating them too. Try chopping up some orange segments, putting them in ice-cube trays, adding fresh orange juice to cover, then freezing.

americano

The Americano is a refreshing blend of bitter and sweet, topped with soda, making the perfect thirst-quencher.

25 ml Campari

25 ml sweet vermouth

soda water, to top up

an orange slice, to garnish

a highball glass

Serves 1

Build the ingredients over ice into a highball glass, then stir and serve with an orange slice.

By adding strawberries to this vibrant cocktail, the rum flavour is not so strong and the drink is a little sweeter.

dark and strawmy

50 ml dark rum

3 lime wedges

2 strawberries, sliced

ginger beer

a highball glass

Serves 1

Muddle the lime and the strawberries in a highball glass. Add ice and the remaining ingredients and stir gently. Serve with two straws.

watermelon and strawberry cooler

This is one of the easiest and most refreshing summer drinks to make, but you do really need to use a juicer.

1 large watermelon

500 g strawberries, hulled, plus extra to garnish

1 unwaxed lemon, peeled and chopped

100 ml vodka (optional)

3 sprigs of fresh mint, leaves roughly torn

a juicer

6–8 highball glasses

Serves 6–8

Cut the watermelon in half, then cut off a thin slice for garnishing. Scoop out the pulp and cut into rough chunks. Feed the watermelon, strawberries and lemon chunks through the juicer alternately. Put ice cubes into a jug (plus the vodka, if using). Pour over the juice. Add the mint and stir well. Pour into the glasses and decorate with a slice of watermelon and a few slices of strawberry to serve.

exotic sea breeze

A variation on the classic cocktail, with pomegranate giving an exotic twist.

200 ml vodka

400 ml pomegranate juice

300 ml ruby grapefruit juice

100 ml freshly squeezed juice from 2–3 limes

2–3 teaspoons pomegranate syrup

1 pomegranate, halved and sliced

a few sprigs of fresh mint

Serves 6–8

Pour the vodka, pomegranate juice, ruby grapefruit juice and lime juice into a large jugful of ice. Sweeten to taste with pomegranate syrup. Garnish with pomegranate seeds and sprigs of mint to serve.

fruit and herb pimm's

A balmy summer's evening seems the perfect time for a glass of Pimm's, overflowing with soft fruits and fresh herbs. You can vary the fruits as you wish, but always include some slices of cucumber and a handful of fresh mint leaves.

1 bottle Pimm's No 1

250 g strawberries, hulled and halved

1/2 melon, deseeded and chopped, or nectarine slices

1 unwaxed lemon, sliced

1/2 cucumber, sliced

a few fresh mint leaves

lemonade or ginger ale, to serve

Serves 12

Pour the Pimm's into a large jug and add the halved strawberries, nectarine slices, lemon slices, cucumber slices and some mint leaves. Set aside to infuse for 30 minutes. Pour into tall glasses filled with ice cubes and top up with lemonade or ginger ale.

The refreshing lime and fresh mint flavours of this traditional Cuban cocktail mask the kick of the rum.

mojito

2 lime wedges

2 barspoons granulated sugar

8 sprigs of fresh mint, plus 1 to garnish

50 ml white rum

1 dash soda water

crushed ice

sugar syrup, to taste (page 140)

a highball glass

Serves 1

Muddle the lime, sugar and mint in the bottom of a highball glass, fill with plenty of crushed ice and add the rum. Stir well and add a dash of soda water. Add a dash or two of sugar syrup, to taste. Garnish with a mint sprig and serve.

The classic vodka and lime combination has been given a refreshing twist with a few drops of Angostura bitters.

iced long vodka

4 shots iced vodka

4 shots lime cordial

a few drops of Angostura bitters

tonic water, to serve

1 unwaxed lemon, sliced, to serve

Serves 4

Pour the vodka, lime cordial and a little Angostura bitters into 4 tall glasses and add ice cubes and lemon slices. Top up with tonic water and serve.

sparkling sea breeze

Although the ingredients are available year-round, this refreshing sparkling cocktail works particularly well at a summer party.

200 ml cranberry-flavoured vodka, chilled

250 ml grapefruit juice, chilled (use pink grapefruit juice if your vodka is colourless)

1 bottle sparkling wine or Champagne, 750 ml, well chilled

Serves 8–10

Pour the cranberry vodka and grapefruit juice into a large jug and mix well. Add the sparkling wine, stir gently, then slowly pour into the glasses.

This cocktail was named after the big artillery gun that terrorized the Germans during the First World War. A popular variation on this drink was to mix Cognac with the Champagne.

french 75

20 ml gin

10 ml freshly squeezed lemon juice

1 barspoon sugar syrup (page 140)

Champagne, to top up

lemon zest, to garnish

Serves 1

Shake the gin, lemon juice and sugar syrup over ice and strain into a champagne flute. Top with Champagne and garnish with a long strip of lemon zest.

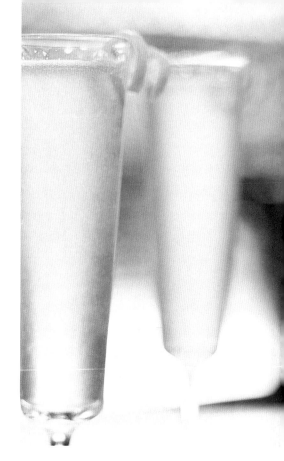

fresh strawberry sparkler

A simple idea, but a hugely pretty one.

1 ripe medium strawberry, hulled and thinly sliced

a little sugar syrup, to taste (page 140)

125 ml rosé Champagne or other pink sparkling wine, well chilled

Serves 1

Put the sliced strawberry in the glass, add a dash of sugar syrup to taste and top up with rosé Champagne.

fresh passionfruit fizz

This makes a romantic cocktail for two.

2 passionfruit (choose ones with slightly wrinkly skin)

2–4 teaspoons passionfruit liqueur, such as Alizé, or passionfruit syrup

cava or other inexpensive sparkling wine, well chilled

Serves 1

Scoop the passionfruit pulp into a small sieve and press it through the holes, scraping a knife over the bottom of the sieve to ensure you collect all of it. Spoon it into 2 chilled glasses, add the passionfruit liqueur or syrup, depending on how sweet your passionfruit is, and slowly top up with fizz.

classic bellini

The bellini was invented at Harry's Bar in Venice. It is traditionally made with white peaches and prosecco, but you could equally well use yellow peaches and Champagne.

about 60 ml freshly made white peach juice (from 1 large chilled peach)

prosecco or Champagne, well chilled

2 teaspoons peach-flavoured liqueur, well chilled (optional)

Serves 1

Pour the peach juice to just under halfway up the champagne flute and slowly top up with chilled fizz. Stir carefully and taste, adding a little peach liqueur if you think the peach flavour needs intensifying.

Variation You can make a bellini with many different kinds of freshly juiced fruit: raspberry, strawberry, mixed strawberry and watermelon, and pear are all good. Some fruits are more intense than others – you'll need less raspberry juice, for instance, than you would peach or pear juice. Some fruits, such as peaches and pears, discolour quickly so use them immediately or add a little lemon juice to stop them turning brown.

The ginger combines conspiratorially with the Champagne to create a cocktail that is delicate yet different.

ginger champagne

2 thin peeled fresh ginger slices

25 ml vodka

Champagne, to top up

a cocktail shaker

Serves 1

Put the ginger in a cocktail shaker and press with a barspoon or muddler to release the flavour. Add ice and the vodka, shake and strain into a champagne flute. Top with Champagne and serve.

It is thought that Alfred Hitchcock invented this drink some time during the 1940s in an old San Francisco eatery called Jack's. He devised it for a group of friends who were suffering from hangovers.

mimosa

1/2 glass Champagne

10 ml Grand Marnier

freshly squeezed orange juice, to top up

Serves 1

Pour the orange juice over the Champagne and Grand Marnier and stir gently.

Index

recipe credits

GHILLIE BASAN
Almond milk
Lemon couscous with roast vegetables
Roast chicken stuffed with couscous, apricots and dates

FIONA BECKETT
Butterflied leg of lamb with cumin, lemon and garlic
Classic bellini
Exotic sea breeze
Fresh passionfruit fizz
Fresh strawberry sparkler
Ham and melon platter
Homemade lemonade
Kisir
Lavender shortbread
Mini pissaladières
Old-fashioned white wine cup
Seared tuna with tomatoes, rocket and gremolata
Sicilian-spiced seabass with grilled tomatoes and baby fennel
Sparkling nectarine and blueberry jellies
Sparkling sea breeze
Sparkling Shiraz and summer berry jellies
Sun-dried tomato, olive and basil bread
Watermelon and strawberry cooler

SUSANNAH BLAKE
Meringues with rosewater cream

MAXINE CLARK
Quiche Lorraine
Raisin and aniseed cake
Sardenaira
Tomato upside-down tart

ROSS DOBSON
Figs with crispy prosciutto, blue cheese and rocket
Mozzarella, peach and frisée salad

CLARE FERGUSON
Apricot tart
Asparagus with prosciutto
Beggar's caviar
Camargue rice salad
Chicken sauté Provence-style
Dried tomato purée
Fennel and orange salad
French lemon tart
Gazpacho Pedro Ximenez
Green olive and basil paste
Italian bean dip
Peaches in rose syrup
Provençal tomatoes
Red leaf salad
Salade Niçoise
Scented fruit jelly
Spanish potato omelette
Spanish tart with peppers
Stuffed Greek aubergines
Sugared strawberries
Tapenade

LIZ FRANKLIN
Lemon yoghurt ice cream
Summer berry yoghurt ice cream

TONIA GEORGE
Blackberry tea vodka
Chai vanilla milkshake
G & tea
Green tea martini
Iced peach and elderflower tea
Moroccan fresh mint tea

BRIAN GLOVER
Lemon, thyme and green tea sorbet with pistachio and lemon wafers

JANE NORAIKA
Aubergine and smoked cheese rolls
Chilled avocado and pepper soup
Coriander flatbreads with spiced aubergines and split pea dip
Leek, feta and black olive tart with endive and watercress salad and spiced walnuts
Chargrilled dill polenta with lemon, fennel and spring onions
Pan-grilled strawberries
Roasted vegetable and ricotta loaf
Strawberry and mascarpone trifle
Stuffed focaccia bread
Summer brioche pudding
Tofu in a hot, sweet and spicy infusion

ELSA PETERSEN-SCHEPELERN
Apple lemonade
Jamaican iced ginger sorrel tea
Jamaican punch

LOUISE PICKFORD
Text on page 7
Barbecue duck ricepaper rolls
Barbecued artichokes with chilli lime mayonnaise
Barbecued pears with spiced honey, walnuts and blue cheese
Barbecued rosemary flatbread
Beetroot and baby onion brochettes
Best-ever beef burger
Broad bean salad with mint and Parmesan
Bruschetta with caramelized garlic
Charred leeks with tarator sauce
Chicken Caesar wrap
Chicken panini with roasted pepper and rocket aïoli
Chicken salad with radicchio and pine nuts
Courgette, feta and mint salad
Dukkah-crusted tuna with preserved lemon salsa
Ember-roasted potatoes
Fig, goats' cheese and prosciutto skewers with radicchio salad
Fruit and herb Pimm's
Garlic bread skewers
Ginger and lime cordial
Grilled figs with almond mascarpone cream
Grilled fruit parcels
Grilled pita salad with olive salsa and mozzarella
Hot-smoked Creole salmon
Iced ginger tea
Iced lemon coffee
Iced long vodka
Indonesian chilli fruit salad
Japanese garden salad with noodles
Kiwifruit, passionfruit and lime sticky
Lamb burgers with mint yoghurt
Lime and mint stick drink
Mango cheeks with spiced palm sugar ice cream
Mini pork and apple pies
Mixed mushroom frittata
Moroccan fish skewers with couscous
Mushroom burgers with charred chilli mayonnaise
Onion, thyme and goats' cheese tarts
Orange and soy-glazed duck
Orzo salad with lemon and herb dressing
Oysters with spicy chorizo
Pasta, squash and feta salad with olive dressing
Pepper 'n' spice chicken
Peppered tuna steak with salsa rossa
Prawn and beef satays
Prawn, chorizo and sage skewers
Red snapper with parsley salad
Roquefort and walnut tart
Smoky barbecue ribs
Souvlaki with cracked wheat salad
Squid piri-piri
Steak with blue cheese butter
Strawberry, pear and orange frappé
Stuffed picnic loaf
Summer vegetables with bagna cauda
Thai-style beef salad
Three salsas
Toasted coconut ice cream with grilled pineapple
Vietnamese pork balls
Whole beef fillet with mushrooms
Whole chicken roasted on the barbecue
Whole salmon stuffed with herbs

BEN REED
Americano
Dark and strawmy
Diablo
French 75
Ginger champagne
Herba Buena
Mimosa
Mojito
Raspberry rickey

FIONA SMITH
Piquant goat's cheese and grilled red pepper terrine

SUNIL VIJAYAKAR
Kiwi and stem ginger sorbet
Orange and lemon granita
Pomegranate granita
Star anise and mandarin granita

FRAN WARDE
Baked aubergines with pesto
Barbecued courgettes
Bean and mint salad
Chicken and tarragon pesto pasta
Coconut and passionfruit shortbread bake
Crab spaghetti with chilli mussels
Easy fish stew
Korean chicken
Leaf and herb salad

Lime mousse with lemon sauce
Lobster salad with chilli dressing
Nectarine tart
Orange and lemon bake with minted yoghurt
Prawn noodle broth
Rosemary and lemon roasted chicken
Sage-stuffed pork fillet with puy lentils and spring onion dressing
Seasonal fruit tarts
Sesame-crusted marlin with ginger dressing
Ginger lemonade
Strawberry tart
Summer salad
Sweet glazed pepper salad
Swordfish with salsa
Tea-smoked trout with cucumber salad
Toasted ciabatta pizzas
Turkish toasted bread
Turmeric lamb fillet with couscous salad
White wine spritzer

LINDY WILDSMITH
Aromatic pork burger in pita bread
Bloody Venetian
Blueberry frangipane tart
Chilled spinach, rocket and watercress soup
Hot crusty loaf filled with mozzarella, salami and tomato
Layered salmon, prawn and potato filo pie
Pineapple and thyme loaf cake
Risotto with Sicilian pesto
Traditional English apple tart
Virginia mint julep

---

photography credits

KEY: a=above, b=below, r=right, l=left, c=centre.

JAN BALDWIN
Pages 4 (Camp Kent designed by Alexandra Champalimaud www.alexchamp.com), 10l, 24l (Suzy & Graham Hursts' house in Palm Beach, Sydney, New South Wales), 30b, 91b, 127l (designed by Stephen Blatt Architects www.sbarchitects.com), 149ar, 149bc (www.alexchamp.com as before), 155l (interior designer Philip Hooper's home in East Sussex) 157l (Laurence & Yves Sabourets' house in Brittany), 166l

MARTIN BRIGDALE
Pages 8, 17l, 27, 28, 30ar, 31, 35, 38a, 46a, 79r, 82, 84, 87, 89a, 91a, 96, 99, 115al, 118 both, 119, 128, 130, 131 all, 134l, 155r, 157r, 158l, 160, 161

PETER CASSIDY
Pages 9ar, 11, 13a, 14a, 15, 22, 32, 39r, 41a, 41br, 46b both, 74, 92, 97 both, 102 both, 103, 104 both, 107, 110, 114, 115ac, 116, 124, 126l, 137, 138r, 139, 140 both, 141 all, 149bl, 151, 154, 163r, 167r, 172l

CHRISTOPHER DRAKE
Page 90a (Maurizio Epifani, owner of L'oro dei Farlocchi/www.lorodeifarlocchi.com)

STYLED BY ENRICA STABILE:
Pages 1-3, 6, 29l, 38b (Siegliende Wondert's terrace in Milan) 39l, 51ac, 53a (a Soho roof top New York), 57r (garden designer Mary Z. Jenkins's house in New York), 89b, 101 inset, 106l
Enrica Stabile, antiques dealer, interior decorator and photographic stylist:
L'Utile e il Dilettevole (shop)
Via Carlo Maria Maggi 6
20154 Milano
+39 0234 53 60 86
www.enricastabile.com

RICHARD JUNG
Pages 42a, 49l, 85, 142 both, 144, 145 both

WILLIAM LINGWOOD
Pages 21, 24r, 30al, 53b, 54r, 55, 88l, 94, 117, 122, 133, 146a, 147r, 156 both, 162, 163l, 164r, 166r, 169, 170r, 173

PAUL MASSEY
Pages 17r, 18l, 20a (the home in Denmark of Charlotte Lynggaard, designer of Ole Lynggaard Copenhagen/www.olelynggaard.dk), 41bl, 76l, 79l(Hôtel Le Sénéchal, Ars en Ré, designed by Christophe Ducharme Architecte/www.hotel-le-senechal.com), 134r, 147l, 152r (the Barton's seaside home in West Sussex: www.thedodo.co.uk), 159r, 167l

JAMES MERRELL
Page 164l

CLAIRE RICHARDSON
Page 172r

DEBI TRELOAR
Pages 5, 9ac, 14b, 23, 33al, 33ac, 34 both, 37 both, 44b, 45l, 48 both, 51al, 52a, 63 both, 64 both, 77l, 83ar, 88r, 95 all, 98all, 100, 101 main, 106r, 108, 109 both, 113, 115ar, 120l (Riad Chambres d'Amis in Marrakech (B&B), designed and owned by Ank de la Plume, decorated in co-production with Household Hardware and Rutger Jan de Lange: www.chambresdamis.com), 121, 125 all, 126r, 129 both, 135 both, 138l, 146b (www.chambresdamis.com as before), 148, 149al, 150, 165, 170l

CHRIS TUBBS
Endpapers, pages 83al (Vanni & Nicoletta Calamai's home near Siena), 83c (Toia Saibene & Giuliana Magnifico's home in Lucignano, Tuscany), 83b (designer Gabriella Cantaluppi Abbado's home in Monticchiello +39 333 90 30 809), 86a (Toia Saibene & Giuliana Magnifico's home in Lucignano, Tuscany)

IAN WALLACE
Pages 9al, 9b, 10r, 13b, 16, 18r, 19, 20b, 25 both, 26, 29r, 33ar, 33b, 36, 42b, 43, 44a, 45r, 47, 49r, 50, 51ar, 51b, 52b, 54l, 56 both, 57l, 58, 59 both, 60, 61, 62, 65, 66, 67 both, 68, 69, 70, 71 all, 72, 73, 75, 76r, 77r, 78 both, 80 both, 81, 86b, 90b, 93, 105, 111 both, 112, 115b, 120r, 123, 127r, 132, 136, 143, 149br, 152l, 153, 158-159, 168 both, 171